I0867769

BOB BYRNE

AUSTRALIA

Remember this too!

NEWSOUTH

For my wife, Helen
For my children, Catherine, Anthony and Alison
And my grandchildren, Harrison and Jasmine

FOREWORD

This is the second book featuring the most popular nostalgia posts and photos from the 'Australia Remember When' Facebook page and website.

As I wrote in the first volume *Australia Remember When*: 'It is not meant to be an historical account of growing up in Australia, but rather a nostalgic look back at some of the moments, events, people, personalities and places that were part of an era from the '50s to the '80s, the Baby Boomer years.'

Since that first book was published in 2015 the Facebook page has continued to grow and at the time of writing was approaching 125 000 'Likes' with over 120 000 regular followers and contributors. Each day thousands of people view, share, 'like' and comment on each post. Nostalgia, it seems, is more popular than ever.

Some of the posts, reproduced in this book, have gone viral and attracted upwards of half a million views, something I would never have believed could happen when I started the page back in 2013.

Australia Remember This Too! is a snapshot of an age, the 'Kodak' moments of a generation, reminders from a different time and a different country. And they're the little things, the simple experiences, objects and events we all shared and that have now all but vanished, consigned to the dustbin of history.

Many of the photos that appear on these pages come from our readers' personal collections, sharing their special memories about which they love to reminisce.

It's a popular theory that as we age we tend to look back at the past through rose-tinted glasses. Time has a way of softening memories and in contrast to our busy and sometimes more complicated lives of today, it can often feel like things were much simpler 'back then'.

Whether that's true or not may be open for discussion but one thing is for sure – these are our stories and memories to share with our children and grandchildren; family tales to connect generations with the past, present and future.

My hope for this book is that it will revive a long-lost memory for you, bring the joy and happiness of a forgotten but treasured moment from your life and create a lively discussion between families members about the 'good old days'.

The best birthday parties had fairy bread and lots of raspberry cordial.

thecattylife.com

Remember when, as a kid, your birthday party was just a simple neighbourhood affair?

My grandchildren seem to be at a birthday party almost every weekend, most times held at a professional venue and costing God knows what.

Whenever there was a birthday celebrated back in the day, there would be a party for all the neighbourhood kids because school friends mostly lived too far away. There'd be raspberry cordial to drink, little cakes in patty pans, chocolate crackles and fairy bread with hundreds and thousands. The decorations were all usually handmade with crepe paper and there'd be a little paper trumpet to blow. There'd be games too such as 'Pass the Parcel' and 'Pin the Tail on the Donkey'.

All pretty simple compared to today's kid's parties ... I'll bet the kids still love fairy bread, though.

In South Australia we used to call these 'dandies' but I've heard them called 'Dixies'. They were small tubs of ice cream and you ate them with a little wooden spoon. We sometimes had a Dixie Cup at the pictures on Saturday afternoon

Gosh, that brings back memories from so long ago!

A real treat at the pictures was a little tub of ice cream with its own little wooden spoon.

State Library of Western Australia, 128133PD

1934

Remember the excitement when you got a free one?

Courtesy of the Daily Juice Company

A Sunny-boy was one of the great favourites from the school tuck shop.

Sunny-boy was orange flavoured, Razz was raspberry and Glug was sort of cola-flavoured. And if you found the words 'Sunny-boy Free Drink' inside, you got a free one!

A few years ago now the Daily Juice Co. confirmed that it had ceased production of the pyramid-shaped frozen treats due to a 'sustained reduction in consumer demand' over time.

'The Daily Juice Co. can confirm that we have regrettably had to make the hard decision to stop production of the icy treat, Sunny-boy, as of August 2016,' a spokesperson for the company said. 'Unfortunately, Sunny-boy has experienced a sustained reduction in consumer demand over a long period of time, making it necessary to delete the product from our range of water ice treats.'

#1 FACT

Swimming costumes in Queensland are known as togs and cossies in NSW, but in Victoria and South Australia they're bathers. And while Victorians use the word cantaloupe, in the rest of the country the fruit is known as rockmelon.

In summer we would head for the beach or the nearest public swimming pool. It was the only way to keep cool before air-conditioning.

Photo by News Ltd/Newspix

Before the advent of backyard swimming pools, when summer arrived we'd head for the beach or the public swimming pool. Whether you lived in the city or in a country town there was usually a public pool and during school holidays they were always crowded with kids learning to swim or just trying to keep cool.

Some of the pools also had a diving tower and the big kids would climb the tallest tower and dive bomb into the pool. How there weren't more accidents I'll never know.

The public pools were also the centre of my greatest fear and loathing, the annual school swimming carnival ... hated it, loathed it because I was a real dunce when it came to swimming.

What are your memories of summer at the public swimming pool?

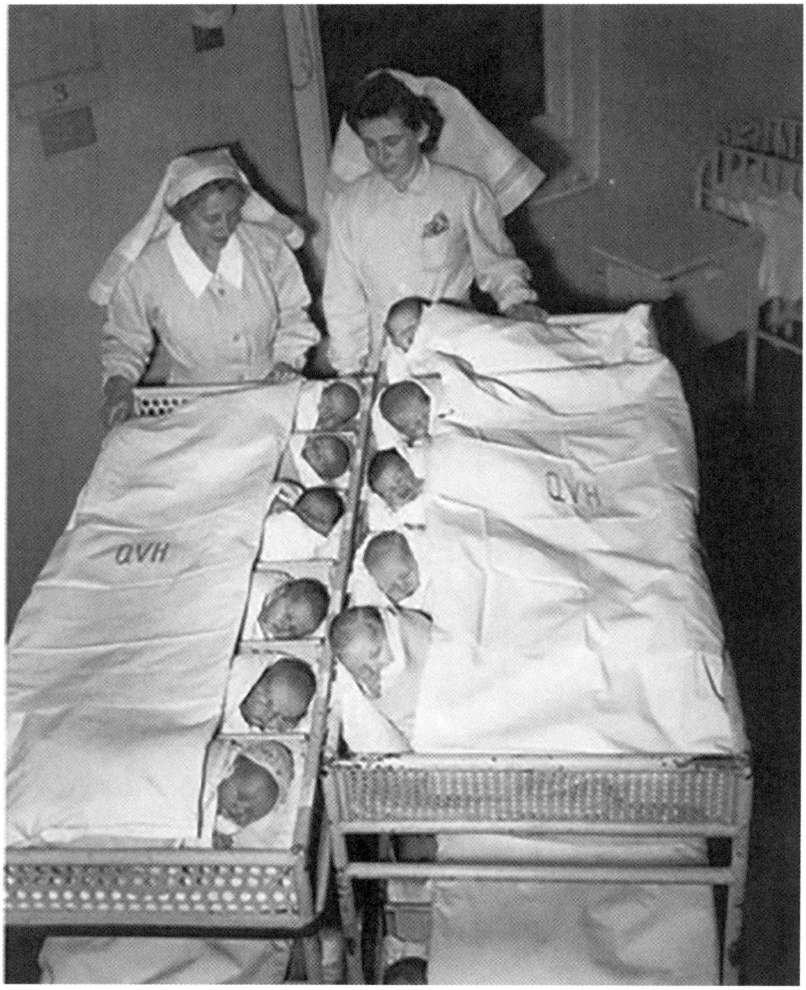

Newly born and off to the nursery with all the other babies. No such thing as 'early bonding' in the '40s and '50s.

Source unknown

When a baby was born in hospital in the '50s and right up to the early '70s, it was whisked away to the hospital nursery where it was placed in a crib along with all the other newborns and only delivered back to the mother to be breast fed or bottle fed.

It seems so amazing in today's more caring environment of early bonding that it was less than 50 years ago that fathers were completely excluded from anything to do with the birth of their child and could only look at their newly born son or daughter through a window in the nursery as the nurse held it up.

My eldest daughter was born in 1972 at Gosford in NSW, and while I was at the birth I was not able to nurse my baby until she arrived home from hospital a week later.

There was a time when nurses learned their craft while on the job. My sister started as a nurse's aide, studied hard, took exams and finally qualified as a registered nurse.

State Library of New South Wales, Mitchell Library, Government Printing Office 2-11237

There was a time when nurses had a strict uniform code and lived in 'The Nurses Quarters'?

My sister spent some years as a nurse in the 1960s, starting out as a 'nurse's aide' and gradually passed through the various levels until she was fully qualified. We recently reminisced about those years and she reminded me of some of her duties back then. She did everything from emptying bed pans through to 'laying out' the bodies of patients who died in her ward.

A nurse's life was completely controlled by the 'Matron' who ruled the hospital with an iron fist in those days. Nurses were strictly supervised at all times and were reqired to be in their quarters every night by 10 pm.

Before the big hardware chains arrived, most of Australia's hardware shops were small businesses run by families. Remember you could buy a single bolt and nut, a single tap washer, nails were sold by the pound and the advice was given free?!

There were wheelbarrows by the front door, ladders down the back and the key-cutting machine was generally whirring in the background. There were rows and rows of bits and pieces and the people behind the counter could put their hand straight on whatever you wanted.

I used love that smell, hard to describe, but it was so distinctive that you knew you were in the hardware store.

Sadly, most are now gone, replaced by the big chains and everything is pre-packaged, it's all self-serve and finding assistance or advice is next to impossible.

Remember when you had a local hardware shop?

The corner hardware shop had everything you ever needed for those DIY jobs and the advice was free.

Wikipedia, photo Joe Mabel

Keystone

When we were kids we could never get enough of plasticine.

If I close my eyes and think about it now I can still smell it. Plasticine allowed you to be super creative and we would make all sorts of animals, people, objects and also unnamed, weird creations that when you realised how strange they were, you simply rolled them back into a ball and started again.

Occasionally when you'd get a new box of plasticine (maybe for Christmas), all the colours were still separate and you could really come up with some great models but it wouldn't be long before they were all rolled into one big ball, which from memory was a dirty green colour, sometimes with slight traces of the other colours.

I guess plasticine is still around although I hear more about Play-Doh these days (I don't think we had Play-Doh).

What are your memories of plasticine when growing up?

I loved getting a new box of Placistine in all the different colours. After some use and when they were all mixed together it went a sort of grey-green colour – usually including hair!

Pinterest

Mike Willesee had the top-rated current affairs TV programme in the 1970s.

Photo by News Ltd/Newspix

Back in the '70s, Mike Willesee's *A Current Affair* was compulsory viewing every night.

It started in 1971, screening week nights at 7 pm, and was broadcast on Channel 9. Mike was a great interviewer and I well remember some of his feisty clashes with Gough Whitlam, Bob Hawke, Malcolm Fraser and other political leaders of the day.

His most memorable series of interviews included those with Quentin Kenihan, pictured here, who became something of a national celebrity.

Mike left Nine in 1974 to move to the rival 0–10 Network, and after several presenters, *A Current Affair* was cancelled in 1978.

In 1984, Willesee returned to the Nine Network to revive the format in a series titled *Willesee*, which then continued running five nights a week until 1988, when Willesee's production company, Transmedia, sold the rights to the program to the Nine Network.

A Current Affair these days is nothing like the program of those early years.

#2 FACT

Did you know that there are almost 100 000 more women than men in Australia? And there are now more people in Sydney who were born in China as opposed to England. Australia's population is now 25 million and growing by 500 000 a year.

Col Joye and Judy Stone were top of the pops when rock 'n' roll first arrived in Australia in the late 1950s.

Judy was born in 1942 and came to national prominence in the late 1950s through her regular TV appearances on Brian Henderson's *Bandstand*. Major national hits were 'I'll Step Down' (1962), '4,003,221 Tears From Now' (1964), 'Born a Woman' (1966), '(Would You Lay with Me) in a Field of Stone' (1974), 'Mare Mare Mare' (1974), 'Hasta Mañana' (1976) and 'Silver Wings & Golden Rings' (1976). In 2006 she was awarded the Member of the Order of Australia, with the citation, 'For service to the community as an entertainer at fundraising events for a range of charitable organisations, and as a singer.'

Col Joye experienced a string of chart successes in the early Australian rock 'n' roll scene and was the first Australian rock 'n' roll singer to have a number one record Australia-wide with 'Oh Yeah Uh Huh'. Recording solo and with his backing band The Joy Boys, he had a string of hits beginning in 1959.

For over a decade, Col also appeared regularly on *Bandstand*. He also toured Australia with fellow *Bandstand* acts, including Judy and they often teamed together as a duo on both recordings and on television. 'Heaven Is My Woman's Love' reached No.1 on the *Go-Set* charts in 1973 – his final appearance in the pop music charts.

Col Joye and Judy Stone performing a duo on Brian Henderson's *Bandstand*.

Courtesy of Col Joye and Judy Stone

My Mum used Reckitt's Blue to keep the sheets white and as a cure for bee stings.

Courtesy of Ret on the Net

A strong memory about wash day is when Mum used to 'blue' the water with Reckitt's Blue to wash all the whites.

I could never quite work that out ... Why would you wash something in blue to make it whiter?

According to Wikipedia:

> White fabrics acquire a slight colour cast after use (usually grey or yellow). Since blue and yellow are complementary colours in the subtractive colour model of colour perception, adding a trace of blue colour to the slightly off-white colour of these fabrics makes them appear whiter. Many white fabrics are blued during manufacturing. Bluing is not permanent and rinses out over time leaving dingy or yellowed whites. A commercial bluing product allows the consumer to add the bluing back into the fabric to restore whiteness. On the same principle, bluing is sometimes used by white-haired people in a blue rinse.

A canvas water bag was usually the only way to transport water back in the day.

Courtesy of Geoff Dale, Open ABC

Long before we carried around plastic bottles of very expensive 'spring' water, there was the old canvas water bag!

Every home had one of these, although I haven't seen one for a long time.

Remember how you could buy a water bag holder that you screwed on to the front

There was a saying about 'taking a Bex and having a lie-down' back in the '50s and '60s but many housewives of the day chose the pink Vincent's Powders instead.

Both products became Australian cultural icons, prominent among this country's repertoire of self-prescribed, over-the-counter medications, popular in the mid-20th century. While everyone knew that the combination of aspirin, phenacetin and caffeine in Bex and Vincent's Powders was used by Australian housewives to help them get through the day, it took a doctor from South Africa in the 1960s, Priscilla Kincaid-Smith, to recognise that these substances were addictive and that the massive doses of phenacetin taken by habitual users was causing widespread kidney disease. Eventually, government controls were put on analgesic products in the 1970s.

Do you remember your mum or grandma taking a Vincent's or Bex everyday?

Housewives of the '50s and '60s became hooked on Vincent's or Bex powders.

Courtesy of Peter's Milk Bar

bumper bar for when the family was going on a car trip? It was the only way we carried water for the whole family ... Mum would have those little aluminium anodised cups in a zip-up leather pouch and would hand one to each child for our drink when we stopped for petrol. No soft drinks were ever considered!

What are some of your favourite things from the past? Toys, gadgets, inventions, places, bands, people, etc.?

I remember playing for hours with my humming top, which had a sort of plunger that you'd have to pump up and down to get the top spinning – and it would hum. There was also a smaller kind that you wrapped the string around and sort of threw, keeping it low to the floor. That thing would spin for the longest time! Finally, it would start to slow and wobble and fall over. Then the process starts all over: wrap the string and ...

When I was a kid, we had to work for our entertainment! LOL!

A 'humming' top was always a toy favourite for Baby Boomers.

eBay

Betsy McCall, the famous paper doll with brother Sandy and sister Barbara.

Courtesy Betsy of McCall

Who remembers McCall's famous paper doll, Betsy?

I recall my sisters playing with and dressing their paper dolls way back in the '50s. From memory I never got to be in their games but I do recollect the pages of the magazine with the cut-out doll and the cut-out clothes with the little tabs.

This is from the Global Toy News website:

In 1951, McCalls magazine, a popular periodical aimed at housewives, introduced Betsy McCall, a paper doll of a sweet young girl with many outfits and accessories. McCalls also distributed Betsy sets for mail-order sales. In 1955, the company offered a set that included Betsy, her parents, brother, and pet dog named Nosy. Although McCalls ran the last of the Betsy series in 1995, she remains a popular collector's item.

Pauline Florence sent me this photo of those little tins of dressmaker pins, remember those?

'They were a very common sight at home and remind me of my dear mum, sitting at the kitchen table mending clothes, darning socks and sewing,' Pauline wrote

That reminds me that in pre-TV days we'd all sit around listening to the wireless and when TV arrived at our house in the late '50s, we'd all sit together on the lounge, in a darkened room, so no more mending!

It would still have been done, but changed from nights to sometime during the day, most likely.

These little pin tins were a common sight around the home back in the day.

Courtesy of Pauline Florence

Gillian Perkins posted a memory: 'Wooden thread spools, memories. When the cotton was finished, we placed four small nails on top ... it was then a knitting nancy.'

My Grandma would nail four tacks into the top of the wooden spool and start our knitting nancy for us. In South Australia they were also known as 'tomboys'.

It was something we all did as kids at school, both boys and girls, and I believe that kids today still do it, although there's not too many old wooden cotton reels around anymore!

Remember when cotton came on wooden spools like this?

iStock

The magic of '50s and '60s suburbia when socks were darned, baths shared and kids roamed wild.

Who can remember Mum sitting down listening to the wireless at night and darning all the school socks?

We'd have tea about 6 o'clock, followed by the kids doing the dishes, then settle down with homework and the serials. The kitchen would be warm from the stove still radiating the heat of the fire created to cook the family meal – meat and three veg, and then dessert of bread and butter pudding.

As we laboured away at our times tables, at least once a week, Mum would get out the mending basket and start darning the socks. Memories of an innocent childhood.

A regular chore for my Mum while listening to the wireless at night.

Alamy

1959

#3 FACT

In Australia, the first recorded use of electricity in public took place in Brisbane in 1882. Eight arc lights were lit up along Queen Street, with power supplied by a generator driven by a small engine at Adelaide Street. People stood in groups at the foot of the lamp posts, apparently enjoying the beautiful light.

One of the earliest loyalty programs we ever had. Save all the labels from the Lan-Choo tea packet and you would qualify for a prize.

Museums Victoria. Reg. No: 1008

Marianne Lloyd posted some memories:

> I remember my mother had a jar and she would save the Lan-Choo tea labels – and after many years was able to buy some stainless steel serving plates! Those were the days before tea bags and she would make her tea from loose leaf with a small tea strainer sitting in the cup. The tea strainers were sometimes metal, sometimes plastic and my grandmother used a metal one shaped like an egg, which she would dangle in her cup.

Tracie Leigh Seagrott commented: 'I learnt to dunk my biscuits in this tea! My nan had a huge canister under the kitchen sink of these.'

And Patricia Koopman recalled: 'They even had a catalogue that you could choose your gift from. The more labels one had the better the gift.'

My Mum mainly drank Bushell's tea, and I also remember Amgoorie tea as well. Great memories ... Thanks Marianne.

When I was growing up during the Baby Boomer years, Australians drank tea rather than coffee.

Throughout my childhood and early adolescent years very few people drank coffee whereas everyone drank tea. And I remember my grandmother had some strict rules for making a pot of tea correctly.

Bring the kettle to the boil but don't allow it to boil for too long. Never boil the same water twice. Always rinse the teapot out with the boiling water first – this takes the chill off the teapot. Put in the number of teaspoons equivalent to the number of cups to be poured and then add one for the pot. After adding the hot water, allow the tea to stand for several minutes and always cover with a 'cosy' to keep the heat in. Turn the pot three times and then pour.

And to think these days we just grab a teabag.

My Grandma had some very strict rules about making a pot of tea. Boil the water once, one teaspoon for every cup and one for the pot, cover with the 'cosy' and turn three times before pouring.

Courtesy of Cosy Organic Tea

Biscuits came in big tins and were bought from the grocer. He would ladle them into a brown paper bag and you could buy the broken biscuits, sixpence for a big bag!

Courtesy of Mimmo Cozolino

Before pre-packaging of almost all of our food, there was an age when most things arrived at the corner shop in bulk. There were big sacks of flour, grain and sugar and it was a time when the shop owner or storekeeper would ladle everything into brown paper bags and women always carried a string bag to put their groceries in.

I remember in particular that biscuits would come in a big square tin and there were always some broken biscuits left in the bottom. The shop owner would sometimes reward a child who was shopping with Mum with a few pieces of biscuit or he might decide to sell the damaged stock at a heavily reduced price. I can still recall going to the little corner shop and buying 1/- worth of broken biscuits, and you generally got lots of tasty bits for that amount.

Can you remember buying broken biscuits at the local shop?

These little milk bars/delis were dotted around the city and suburbs. Most are gone now, victims of big suburban shopping centres and supermarkets.

Wikipedia, photo Cnwb

In every suburb and every town around Australia there were these little milk bars/delis with an attached residence where the owners lived.

We had one in the next street to where we lived and they also had the first and only telephone in the neighbourhood. These little shops stayed open after the main shops closed and would often be open for the whole weekend.

I remember on a really hot night we'd sit outside on the front veranda listening to the wireless and Mum would find a shilling for a bottle of cold lemonade from the little shop. What a special treat that was! What memories do you have of the local milk bar/deli?

Here's another favourite from the school tuck shop: who remembers buying a Wizz Fizz sherbet when they had the Disney characters on the pack?

Wizz Fizz is particularly known for its little plastic spoon that allows you to scoop the sherbet powder straight into your mouth right from the packet. That's the way we used to eat it too.

Wizz Fizz packs from 1966 to 1996 had Disney characters, including Mickey Mouse, Donald Duck and Goofy, which were replaced with the characters 'Screaming Mimi', 'Weird Wally', 'Gross Gus', 'Nerdy Neil' and 'Doctor Freak' in 2002. In 2011 the Wizz Fizz packs were relaunched based on a planet theme, with intricate illustrations.

Wizz Fizz has proved an enduring brand. Fyna Foods Australia Pty Ltd produces over 16 million sachets of Wizz Fizz each year in its Melbourne factory.

Wizz Fizz sherbet came in a paper bag with a Disney character on the pack and a little spoon and ring in every pack.

Courtesy of Fyna Foods Australia Pty Ltd

One of the biggest highlights of going to the show was to get your favourite showbag. Even today, all kids love a good showbag.

Pinterest

Roger Lambert posted a memory: 'Who remembers when Showbags at Royal Easter Show were actually sample bags and were free?

I would get a bag that had a small jar of peanut butter in it and walk around the show scooping peanut butter out with my finger.' Nice memories, Roger.

Show bags are apparently one of the main reasons people go to the show and are the most popular item to purchase. Last year there was something like 400 different show bags on sale ranging in price from $2 to $30.

My favourite? Bertie Beetle of course!

#4 FACT

In 1952, when Queen Elizabeth II came to the throne, just 40 Australians reached the age of 100. In 2017, more than 2600 Australians lived until 100 and received a congratulatory message from Her Majesty. An actual telegram from the Queen is a thing of the past.

Full disclosure ... I'm not a royalist and would like to see Australia become a republic ... BUT, you have to admit, no matter what your views on the whole 'head of state' debate, the Queen, as head of the Commonwealth, has served it well for more than half a century. A big job, well done!

And right by her side has been husband Prince Philip, who has now announced his retirement from 'royal' duties.

As Baby Boomers, we have had the Queen as head of state for almost all of our lives. She's always been there, and Philip has been right by her side.

In 1954, the Queen made her first visit to Australia. It was the most extensive tour ever undertaken by any British monarch to this country. In all, she and Philip flew over 16 000 kilometres, taking approximately 33 flights, over 3200 kilometres by road (130 hours in cars in 207 trips), visiting all capitals (except Darwin), and 70 country towns. This extensive travel allowed some 75 per cent of the Australian population to see her at least once during the tour and many Boomers will recall taking part in a very special school welcoming ceremony.

Who remembers that first visit to Australia in 1954? And there have been many since, of course.

For Baby Boomers, Queen Elizabeth and Prince Philip have been part of our lives since birth.

National Library of Australia #PIC/16020/46

When we got our first washing machine it came with an electric wringer, which was an absolute godsend and changed wash days forever.

Courtesy of Andrea Reid

Andrea Reid sent me this photo: 'My mother had one of these.'

Probably 1950s, when we had the new electric wringer. Is it a Hoover, Pope or Simpson? They're the only washing machines I can remember from the era, all manufactured here in Australia of course.

Washing machines were a godsend when they were first introduced and as times have gone on, have improved to the point now where we no longer have a wash day. No need to light the copper, fill the troughs and blue the whites. These days you just throw a load into the washing machine and hang it out to dry!

Once upon a time, glory boxes were a tradition. Some called it a 'hope chest', because it was a symbol of a young woman's hopes and dreams of marriage and setting up her own home.

All sorts of household items were saved in the glory box, the idea being that it would ease the initial expense of setting up a new household. The glory box had the blankets (as per this old *Women's Weekly* ad), other bed linen, towels, tablecloths, cutlery and dishware.

So, whatever happened to glory boxes?

These days, young people move out of home and usually live together before they get married. Then there's ease of purchase: just flash the plastic!

And it would probably be deemed sexist these days.

Just another tradition that's been lost along the way.

When my wife and I got married in the 1970s she had a 'glory box' and in it were all the vital things we needed to set up our new home.

*Courtesy Bauer Media Pty Limited/*The Australian Women's Weekly

Crown of the glory box....
colour-bright.... comfort-right.... Onkaparinga
Choose from a Rainbow of Lifetime Colours
Soft Multi-checks
Blue/Pink/White
Pink/Green/White
Delicate Pastel Checks
Blue/White
Pink/White
Green/White
Plain Pastel Shades
Like this wise bride-to-be you too will delight in the natural healthful warmth and lovely softness of Onkaparinga Pure Wool Blankets. You'll love the wonderful array of colours you can choose from. The gently blended pastel checks ... the glorious self colours. Best of all you'll like the 12 year guarantee, backed by the high standards of quality and workmanship that have made the Onkaparinga label famous with Australian brides for over 89 years.
Choose Onkaparinga
the pure wool BLANKETS you'll love and cherish for a lifetime

The 'double decker' school pencil case with a special rubber (eraser) compartment. These were very popular at my school.

Courtesy of Carnamah Historical Society & Museum, www.carnamah.com.au/toys

Here's something everyone had at school – a pencil case. Some were a bit fancier than others – this one, for example, is made entirely from wood. The lid slides on and off, and the top section swings out to reveal a second level and another pencil case underneath.

I had one like this but I had decorated it over my school years with various doodles and engravings. This photo is from a great collection of old toys and paraphernalia from the '40s/'50s at the Carnamah Historical Society & Museum.

Sheryl Angel sent in a photo that should stir the old memory juices: 'Who can remember their parents doing this to their school pencils? Scraping a thin slice off the end of the pencil with a Stanley knife or a razor blade and writing your name on the pencil. These were found in an old pencil case I had not seen for a while!'

Thanks, Sheryl. I think it was because pencils kept getting lost or left on someone else's desk. I remember my Mum's favourite saying when we needed anything like a new pencil or rubber because we lost one or it had been sharpened down to the stub – 'Do you think I'm made of money?'

Times were much tighter back then and 'every penny saved was a penny earned'. We never went without the necessities but luxuries like a new pencil were rare indeed. Was it the same at your house?

School pencils usually ended up looking just like this.

Courtesy of Sheryl Angel

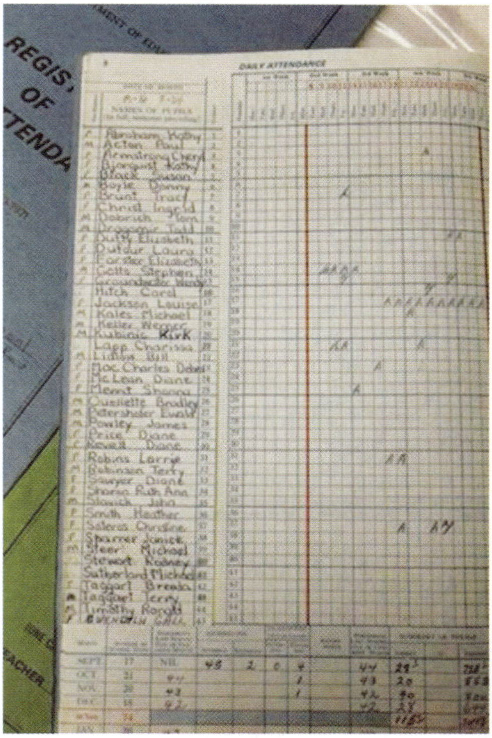

Every morning in class we would have the roll call. All present and correct.

Pinterest

At school there was a roll call. I'm just trying to remember how often we had it. Was it every morning? The teacher would stand out the front of the class and call out students' names one by one and I think we had to put up our hand to show we were in class.

Every Monday was 'school money' day when we took 2/- to school to give to the teacher. I went to a Catholic school so that money was the total cost of our education; as far as I'm aware there were no other costs. I can never remember ever going on a school excursion … I don't believe we had them then.

And it was a great honour to be the class monitor and to take the roll book down to Mother Superior's room.

And who can forget the old Clag glue pot? These days they come in more modern packaging with various means of application, but back in the day we had a pot of glue and a brush which would get very hard with congealed glue as you neared the end of the pot.

And then of course there were those who much preferred Perkins Paste.

I used a bottle just like this for all my school projects.

Clag came with its own brush, which was attached to the lid.

Pinterest

This from 'Adelaide Remember When' Facebook page:

> Anyone who was born in the '50s, '60s, '70s or '80s ... We are the last generation who played in the street. We are the first who played video games, the last to record songs off the radio on a cassette tape. We walked over a mile with no worries of being taken. We learned how to program the VCR before anyone else, we played from Atari to Nintendo, we are the generation of *Tom and Jerry*, *Bugs Bunny* and *Looney Tunes*. We travelled in cars without seat belts or air bags, lived without mobile phones. We didn't have flat screens, surround sound, iPods, Facebook, Twitter, computers or the internet ... But nevertheless we had a great time ... Like and repost if you're a '50s, '60s, '70s or '80s baby.

If you were born in the Boomer years, you were the first to learn how to program a VCR.

Wikipedia, photo Akinom

Video stores – they came and went so quickly. Remember when you'd all go to select the Saturday night movie?

Tracy the astonishing/Flickr

It's amazing to think that the video store has all but disappeared so quickly!

Video came and went all in a matter of 30-odd years. I remember our first VCR, a top-loader that I bought around 1982. By the early 2000s, the VCR was replaced by the DVD, which was only around for a few years – now almost completely replaced by smart TVs and online or streaming movies.

A visit to the old video store on a Friday or Saturday night was always a great experience. There were lots of colourful posters of the latest films available, new movies to be discovered and our local shop had a big range of chocolate treats. Whole families would visit the store, with some kids already dressed in their pyjamas, prepared for a night with loved ones around the TV and then off to bed.

What are your memories of going to the local video store on a Friday or Saturday night?

Helping Mum prepare tea by shelling peas was something we used to do as kids.

With time-poor people and modern food styles, there would be few people today who would have the time and the patience to shell a bowl of peas for the family evening meal.

It was something that my sisters and I were required to do. I still remember Mum, me and my sisters sitting around the table, chatting away and slowly filling the bowl with peas which would then be cooked in a saucepan of water. Strange as it may seem, without all the modern labour saving devices we have today, everyone seemed to have a lot more time.

Plus, it was valuable family communication. We would all sit around talking about things that happened at school that day, what homework we had to do, and as a bonus learned about food preparation and cooking.

Many of those traditional family gatherings have unfortunately been substituted with kids today left to their own devices, playing on their digital gadgets with the family meal often eaten in front of TV.

For many of us, those days of our childhood bring back some wonderful memories and truly treasured moments from the past.

How long has it been since you actually shelled peas? It was part of the regular routine for helping with the preparation of the evening meal.

Courtesy of National Archives of Australia, A1200, L79539

#5 FACT

The Americans may have been the first to put a man on the moon, but Australia received the first clear images. After NASA sent Neil Armstrong, Buzz Aldrin and Michael Collins to the moon on the Apollo 11 mission in 1969, the first signal was received by an antenna at the Honeysuckle Creek Tracking Station in Canberra.

Anyone remember playing on one of these? In the early 1960s the Blue Mountains Council engineer, Mr John Yeaman, visited America and brought back the plans of a playground 'rocket'.

Funded by the Rotary Club of Blackheath, the first Blackheath Rocket was built and installed in the Blackheath Soldiers Memorial Park by Blue Mountains City Council. Over the years the park, like so many other playgrounds, became known to the locals as the 'Rocket Park'.

Dick West, who owned a welding business in Blackheath, went on to make playground rockets that popped up in playgrounds across NSW, Queensland and South Australia. In 1997 the Rocket along with other heritage playground equipment was removed for insurance related issues.

Blackheath Rotary Club have set up a gofundme campaign to raise funds for the new rocket.

These moon rockets were very popular in playgrounds from the '60s through to the '90s but were removed because of safety concerns. I understand they're making a comeback.

Wikipedia, photo Sladew

Rocket Kebabs

I wonder if anyone remembers the Jimmy Sharman Boxing Tent at the Show?

Jimmy Sharman Snr (1887–1965) established his own boxing troupe at a very young age and travelled to about 50 shows a year, the largest being the Sydney Royal Easter Show.

'Who'll take a glove?' and 'A round or two for a pound or two.' (The 'pound' was currency back then). For the next 40 years he remained a fixture of sideshow alley, customers paying their two bob (two shillings) to view fights.

Jimmy Sharman Jnr (1912–2006) was born a year after his father set up his first boxing tent, where Jimmy began working as a teenager.

In 1955 he took over the boxing tent from his father and toured until 1971, when regulations were introduced prohibiting boxers having more than one fight per week. That was the end of the Sharman Boxing Troupe.

For six decades the Sharman tent had followed the show circuit in four states for 11 months each year. Today it is just a memory.

Jimmy Sharman's Boxing Show was a staple at the annual Royal Melbourne Show's sideshow alley.

Photo by News Ltd/Newspix

WORLD CHAMPIONS
AUSTRALIAN CHAMPIONS
YOUNG
JACK DEMPSEY
ROCKY MARCIANO
WHERE AUSTRALIAN CHAMPIONS ARE DISCOVERED
JIMMY SHARMAN'S
TOURING STARS
CONTESTS ARRANGED FOR ALL
LOCAL And DISTRICT CHAMPIONS!
PRIZES TO BE WON BY ALL COMERS
A SPORTING TREAT
FOR MEN - WOMEN
And CHILDREN
6
FOR EVERY CHAMPION FOUND IN THE CITY
ARE DISCOVERED

Jeannie Little made her TV debut on Channel Ten's *Mike Walsh Show* in September 1974. Invited on as a guest showcasing designer maternity clothes, she quickly became a flamboyant regular, with her standard greeting 'Hello Darling!' When the show moved to Channel 9 she became part of the team for the next 15 years.

In 1976 Jeannie won the Gold Logie for most popular television personality and she has won two other Logies for her work on the *Mike Walsh Show*. She was also a regular guest on the *Midday Show* with Ray Martin.

In the late '90s through to the mid-2000s she appeared on the panel discussion show *Beauty and the Beast*.

In February 2011, it was announced that Jeannie was suffering from Alzheimer's disease and was being cared for in a nursing home. In August 2014, family members advised that her illness had advanced to the stage that she 'no longer knows where she is or what's going on around her'.

Jeannie Little – seen here at the 2008 Blacktown Festival – was a TV favourite back on '70s daytime television.

Alamy

Do you recall your Mum making coconut ice for the school fete?

I haven't eaten a piece of coconut ice for donkey's years, but I imagined if I tried it today it would be so sweet!

Coconut ice, chocolate crackles, honey joys, stickjaw toffees, toffee apples ... Who makes these anymore?

One of the treats that Mum would make for the annual school fete.

Amazon

Although never quite as popular as chocolate crackles, these honey joys or honey crackles were right up there on the trading tables at our school fetes.

Seeing this photo of honey joys (crackles) makes me want to go and make a batch, just for old time's sake

Honey joys or honey crackles. A reminder of the school fete.

Pinterest

This is the first (known) recipe for chocolate crackles – a favourite snack for generations of Aussie kids. It appeared in an advertisement in the *Australian Women's Weekly* in December 1937, under the entirely accurate headline 'Gee, they're good!' The ad was placed to plug the vegetable fat Copha, one of the key ingredients of the crackles. The other key ingredient is crispy rice cereal, and in 1953, Rice Bubbles maker Kellogg's nabbed the trademark for 'chocolate crackles' (which it still holds).

In 2003, Kellogg's reportedly stepped over the line when it attempted to (gasp!) trademark the crackles recipe itself. Fortunately, the story was more 'media beat-up' than 'corporate power grab' – it's all but impossible to patent or trademark a recipe.

Chocolate crackles were introduced to the public for the first time in the *Australian Women's Weekly*.

Courtesy Bauer Media Pty Limited/The Australian Women's Weekly

Remember going to town with Mum on a shopping trip to buy a new pair of school shoes?

Shoe departments in the big stores back then smelt of new leather and cardboard. There were always lots of assistants to help with the right size and in some shops they even had an X-ray machine to ensure your feet were correctly fitted. Little did we realise at the time that these machines were a serious health risk because of exposure to radiation.

The shop assistant would regularly disappear into a mysterious back room, only to emerge with even more pairs of shoes to try on. There was much discussion about the 'correct' shoes for 'growing' feet and style and comfort always seemed to come in a distant second and third. I also recall being told, 'Your feet will grow into them', when I complained that the shoes felt too big.

After a great deal of shopping around, and with the shoes finally bought, it was home to let Dad glue on an extra 'Dunlop' sole and heel and tack on little steel heel and toe caps to ensure extra wear.

The annual trip to the shoe shop for the back-to-school shoe fitting, seen here at the Cribb & Foote's shoe department in Ipswich.

John Oxley Library, State Library of Queensland, 102801

Ladies and Childrens Footwear

Enid Blyton was our JK Rowling. She wrote many books and turned many Baby Boomers into avid readers.

Courtesy of Hodder and Stoughton

There was no Harry Potter phenomenon when I was a kid, but there were always lots of books for children including Enid Blyton's *Famous Five* series. I remember a book called *Anthony Thomas on Timothy's Farm* for some reason ... it was one of my childhood favourites.

I later joined the local library and have always been an avid reader. What was your favourite book when you were growing up?

#6 FACT

Perth is the most isolated city in the world. Adelaide is the closest city, and is more than 2000 kilometres away. Perth's King Park, a significant site for Nyoongar heritage, is one of the largest city parks in the world. Perth is also the most isolated capital city in the world, but the isolation is made up for by the fact that it is the sunniest, with an average eight hours of sunshine on any given day.

Remember when we would build a neighbourhood bonfire for cracker night? In South Australia we always celebrated Guy Fawkes night or cracker night on the 5th of November in keeping with the British tradition, while other states had their fireworks celebrations in May each year.

Fire and fireworks always fascinated us when we were kids but these days the politicians and bureaucrats would have a pink fit if you allowed all the kids in the street to build a bonfire and set it alight!

'One night a year, the infinite normality of the suburbs is shot with utter magic' wrote Justin Sheedy in his book *Goodbye Cracker Night*.

ACT Heritage Library

Tuppeny bungers were amazing. You could blow up letterboxes and rubbish bins, though how we ever survived some of the antics we got up to with crackers I'll never know.

What are your strongest memories of cracker night?

Car dashboard from an early Holden.

State Library of South Australia, BRG 213/65/30/34

Car dashboards were pretty simple in the '50s and '60s.

Climbing into the driver's seat of a motorcar these days is almost like entering the cockpit of a jumbo 747. With all the latest digital devices – bluetooth, WiFi, GPS, cruise control, rearview cameras, hands-free parking – and all the other gadgets and gizmos, it's enough to make your head spin.

This is what the first Holden came equipped with in 1948: a speedo, a petrol gauge and temperature gauge. No automatic transmission, no radio, no air-con, just three pedals: clutch, brake and accelerator. Oh, and the dip-switch (remember when that was on the floor too?)

Wanna chewy?

Wrigley Chewing Gum has been a part of everyday life in Australia for over 100 years and in New Zealand for over 90 years.

When we were kids, we'd always be in trouble from either our parents or teachers for chewing gum or blowing bubbles with bubble gum.

I can remember going to the little corner shop and we'd buy a bottle of Coke and put in a chewing gum pellet to make it froth up!

These days I notice that you chew gum after a meal to clean your teeth (according to the ads) so it has become 'dental hygiene'. Not sure why we chewed gum as kids ... Maybe because we could?

From memory I think they were twopence a pack and you got four chewing gum pellets.

Museums Victoria. Reg. No: SH 921176

WRIGLEY'S
AIDS
DIGESTION.
WRIGLEY'S
P.K.
CHEWING GUM
PEPPERMINT FLAVOUR
P.K.

WALTONS
CREDITS LIMITED
$1
Store Credit Certificate
SC 222850
This certificate verifies that Waltons Credits Limited is prepared to guarantee the bearer's credit with WALTONS STORES LIMITED up to the amount endorsed hereon
John B Walton
MANAGING DIRECTOR
WALTONS CREDITS LIMITED
COPYRIGHT

The Waltons man was a familiar figure around the suburbs as he went door-to-door selling white goods, furniture and clothing.

Courtesy of Downies Auctions

Throughout the 1950s – and possibly up to the '70s – the Walton's man called.

Waltons was a department store operating mainly on the east coast of Australia. John Walton opened his first department store in Sydney in 1951 and by 1972, the Waltons chain had expanded to 96 department stores.

Waltons set up a time payment plan long before easy credit plans were available in Australia and targeted thousands of low-to-middle income households. They employed door-to-door salesmen called 'travellers' who sold goods ranging from nappies to lounge suites and white goods, all ordered and delivered by the 'friendly' Waltons man. Problem was that the interest on the credit plan was around 30 per cent and many people struggled to ever pay it off!

Alan Bond bought Waltons in 1981, but the purchase became a financial disaster, with Bond losing $199 million in 1983. When Bond sold Waltons to the Cooke family in 1987 the Waltons department store name disappeared. The Cookes turned the stores into Venture and Norman Ross outlets. Venture went bankrupt in 1994.

Often used as a Christmas stocking filler, sliding number puzzles drove me mad.

eBay

These sliding number puzzles would drive me crazy as I tried to figure out how to get all the numbers into the correct order.

I think we used to get them in Christmas stockings and I remember once getting one in a 'surprise dip'. (Remember those? At the school fete there would be a tub filled with sawdust and little trinkets and games, usually wrapped in newspaper, You'd pay sixpence and dip in and rummage around a bit and pull out your 'prize').

Anyway, I could never get the last two numbers of these puzzles in the right order and they were cleverly designed so you couldn't lift the number out and cheat ... damn!

The other puzzle I hated was the Rubik's Cube ... What diabolically deranged person would inflict such a time-waster on the human race? Dr Rubik, I presume!

The first of the digital games to be released in Australia.

Bob Byrne

Remember the Game & Watch games that were so popular in the '80s?

These handheld electronic games, produced by Nintendo, came out in 1980 and continued to 1991.

They all featured a single game to be played on an LCD screen in addition to a clock, an alarm, or both. The game inspired Nintendo to eventually make the Game Boy.

Titles available in Game & Watch form vary from Mickey Mouse to Balloon Fight, including Nintendo staples such as Donkey Kong, The Legend of Zelda and Mario Bros.

Moulded glass food container and lemon squeezer. Popular in the 1940s and '50s.

Courtesy of Ian Keith Kershaw

Ian Keith Kershaw posted a photo and some memories:

> Who would remember moulded glass items like this lemon squeezer (which we still use) and storage container that would be about one hundred years old? These items were handed down from my grandmother who died in 1945, before my birth.
>
> My mum used to keep the beetroot slices in the green container.
>
> Something small from Australia's past that you won't see new in shops today!

Thanks, Ian. Actually, the green container looks a bit like the butter container that we had at home. My Mum would take the wrapper off a pound of butter and put it on the table under a glass top.

We always ate real butter, never margarine. I don't think my mother trusted margarine; she always used to say 'I know where butter comes from.'

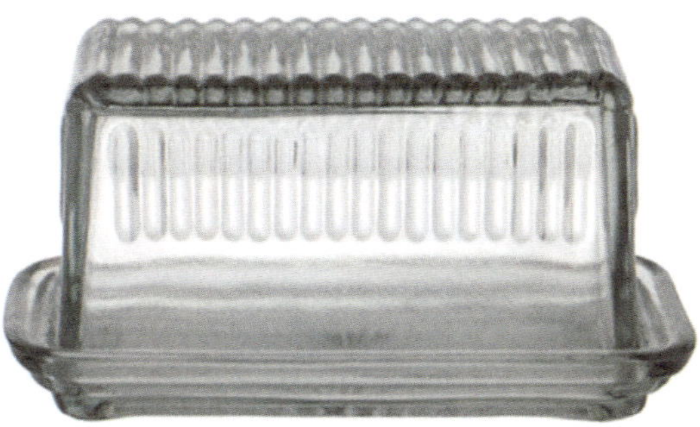

Courtesy of Ian Keith Kershaw

Here is a glass butter dish, similar to one I remember seeing in use when I was a boy. Back then, butter came in a rectangular shape and this moulded glass butter dish was designed to accommodate a full pound!

I inherited many of these items from my parents and they now live in a glass cabinet and are very rarely used.

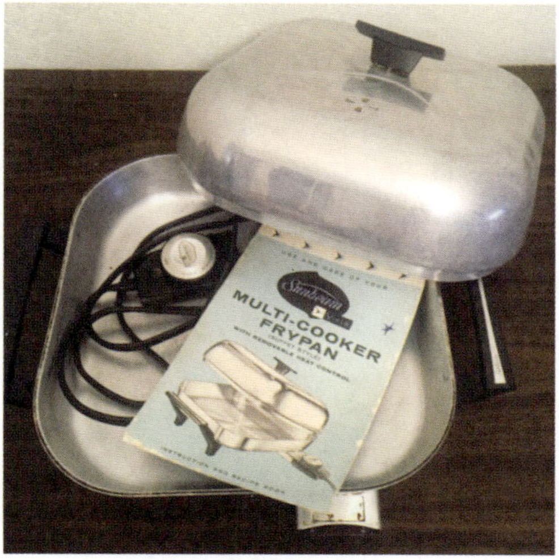

A Sunbeam frypan, a popular cooking item from the 1960s and '70s.

http://ingridmaemusic.blogspot.com

What comes to mind when you look at this photo of an old Sunbeam frypan?

I think back to the time when I first left home as a teenager. I boarded for several years, which is what we did back then, and then a few of the other boarders and I decided we would set up house and look after ourselves.

One of the first things we purchased was a Sunbeam frypan just like this one. I don't think any of us could cook but these electric frypans were pretty simple to use and fortunately quite forgiving of any lack of culinary skill. We all survived some pretty ordinary dishes but fortunately lived to tell the tale.

What are your memories of the electric frypan?

Ian Keith Kershaw sent another photo and some memories:

> Way back in the 1950s these things appeared. They were called Jaffle Irons and with two slices of bread buttered on the outside, filled with baked beans in the middle and toasted in this device you could cook a very simple meal.
>
> I even tried banana with a bit of sugar and had it with ice cream. Yummy!
>
> This one's branded as a Toastie Toaster, so I guess Jaffle Iron may have been the original.
>
> There are now some electric equivalents, some even double.

Great memories, Ian, making 'toasties' in the fire ... although I don't think we called them toasties back then.

'As a child in the 1950s/'60s, my father use to cook jaffles, in the open fire in our lounge room, on cold winter nights on the weekends'.

Courtesy of Ian Keith Kershaw

We learned to roller skate on these adjustable strap-ons. Many skinned elbows and knees before I mastered roller skating.

Courtesy of Sharryn Musk

Sharryn Musk shared a memory: 'It was not easy strapped to our shoes – but fun!'

Thanks, Sharryn – the old original roller skates that we used to strap on over the shoes ... remember those?

I could never quite get the hang of roller skating and never really mastered it. Still have memories of careering around, completely out of control and totally unable to stop, no crash helmet and no elbow or knee pads!

#7 FACT

Originally called Melbourne Rules, Australian Rules Football was first invented to keep cricketers fit in the off season. The very first known game was played in August 1858 between Melbourne Grammar School and Scotch College in Melbourne.

Teresa Glenn shared some memories:

> Does anyone remember playing a game with a rubber ball about the size of a tennis ball, where you threw it against a wall and had to do something else, like clapping your hands or turning around, before you caught it again? I remember playing this game against our garage wall. Then there was tunnel ball, where you had a group of kids in a line and you threw the ball through their legs, and the last person had to grab the ball and run to the front of the line and start again. And of course, who could forget hoppy or its correct name, hopscotch. Wow, we had some fun games ...

Thanks for the memories Teresa.

And they were all outside games too. I clearly recall the game of tunnel ball. Usually played with a basketball it was regular fixture in our school grounds at lunch or recess time.

Another sport we all played at school: tunnel ball. Group games like this were very popular.

Pinterest

One of the more popular games for the girls when I was at school was skipping rope. I remember it was just called 'skippy' and of course there were all sorts of versions, including the double rope. My sisters played this for hours and the boys had a go too. No wonder we were skinny!

There were rhymes that went along with the game and I'm sure some of our readers will remember those.

What skipping rhyme immediately comes to mind?

Here are a couple I remember:

Teddy bear, teddy bear, turn around
[jumper turns while jumping]

Teddy bear, teddy bear, touch the ground
[jumper touches the ground while jumping]

Teddy bear, teddy bear, show your shoe
[jumper thrusts out shoe while jumping]

Teddy bear, teddy bear, [number] to do

1, 2, 3 ... [continues to count to reach the number]

And:

Mable, Mable,
Set the table,
Don't forget the salt,
Vinegar,
Mustard,
Pepper! [rapid turning follows]

'Teddy bear, teddy bear, turn around'. How many skipping rhymes can you still remember?

Alamy

Many of the local drive-in picture theatres had a playground right under the big screen. And all the kids would head for the playground, many dressed in their pyjamas, for a turn on the swing, the seesaw or the slippery dip before it got dark and the film started?

Drive-ins were great family outings back then. Everybody bundled in the car and Mum would have made some sandwiches for tea, or as a special treat we'd be allowed to get a pie or some chips and a Coke from the kiosk at interval.

Remember how Mum would always take a thermos of tea too because it seemed like teatime could never be complete without a nice cup of tea?

The local drive-in had a playground under the big screen for a quick game before the first picture started.

Pinterest

Barbara Rowley shared a memory:

> My Mother had a Singer treadle sewing machine. She made nearly all my clothes when I was growing up. Before going to work one day I left a piece of material for Mum to make me a dress for a dance that night and sure enough when I got home from work there it was all finished. When I had my three girls she made their little nighties and matinee jackets and as they grew she made their little dresses. Unbelievable how fast her legs could move the treadle up and down.

Thanks, Barbara. My Mum was also very handy with the Singer sewing machine. Back then it was something that almost all our mothers learned from their mothers, who had learned from their mothers – how to sew and make children's clothes. Money was pretty tight in our house and this was one way to save, by making the children's clothes when you could.

Almost every kid's mum had a Singer and clothes were often hand-made on a Singer treadle machine.

Alamy

Hand signals used before the introduction of traffic indicators.

Courtesy of Maryann Daniel

My very first car was an Austin A40 and instead of blinkers it had this type of 'semaphore' indicators.

Courtesy of oldclassiccar.co.uk

Before traffic signal indicators were introduced into cars we indicated what we were about to do with hand signals.

Indicators were first introduced around Australia in the 1960s. Before that it was hand signals to indicate if you were turning left, right or stopping.

Maryann Daniel sent this photo of a page from a Queensland driver's instruction manual showing the six hand signals we were all supposed to know. I'm from South Australia and I'm pretty sure we didn't use some of these ... Or was I not giving the correct hand signals back then?

Do you remember all of these?

Bob Harmer sent me this photo with the comment: 'Remember indicators on cars and vans that used to pop out from the centre post between front and back of the car/van? They were called semaphore indicators.'

Thanks, Bob, wow! Yes, I do remember those, in fact I think my first car, a 1949 Austin A40, had them.

From memory they were usually on English-made cars. I believe the earlier Morris Minors had them also.

Don't recall ever seeing them on American or Australian cars. Traffic indicators on cars were introduced in the early '60s.

A Tupperware party in the 1950s.

Alamy

Tupperware arrived in Australia in the '50s and Tupperware parties of the '50s, '60s and '70s soon followed.

The Tupperware party allowed women in the 1950s to work and enjoy the benefits of earning an income while still keeping their main focus on the domestic domain.

In fact, it was during the early '50s that Tupperware's sales and popularity exploded, and that continued through the next two decades.

Tupperware is still a hugely successful company today although the parties are now only part of their marketing mix.

We still have and use a lot of Tupperware at our place – how about you?

In nearly every suburb and country town there was a Saturday afternoon matinee.

Photo by News Ltd/Newspix

Bob Perry posted a photo to share with some memories about the Saturday arvo pictures: 'Remember when the weekend came, there was no school, and on Saturday arvo we'd line up with all the other kids from the neighbourhood at the local picture theatre and pay a shilling for a ticket to the afternoon matinee?'

Back in the day there were always two full-length pictures, an episode of the serial, a cartoon and a *Pete Smith Special*.

The theatre was always packed, with constant noise, regular cat calls and the sound of jaffas rolling down the aisle. It was mayhem, with the ushers and usherettes continually shining torches on noisy groups in an attempt to restore some form of order. Whenever there was any kissing on the screen the whole place would erupt into loud jeers and boos. If there was a projector problem or the film broke, again momentary bedlam, until calm was restored with the film restarting.

Movies today are now just part and parcel of the digital age and can be purchased online for just a few dollars, but back when we went to the flicks on a Saturday afternoon, pictures were something really special and will remain so in our memories.

One of the highlights of the Saturday matinee was at interval.

Pictures would start about 2 pm and after we stood for the national anthem ('God Save the Queen') the pictures would start. At interval time the tray girls and boys would come out with ice creams, lollies and drinks stacked in their trays and after we stocked up with dixie ice creams and jaffas, it was back to our seats ready for the *Heckle and Jeckle* cartoon and then the main picture

Who recalls those from Saturday afternoon matinees?

Saturday matinee at the pictures with the ice cream and lolly trays at interval.

Alamy

#8 FACT

Having occupied this land for at least 60 000 years, Australia's Aboriginal peoples are the oldest surviving culture in the world. They established ways of managing their land and society that were extraordinarily sustainable and ensured good health for all. It is thought that there were between 300 000 to 950 000 Aboriginal people living in Australia when the British arrived in 1788.

As a child I was taken to see the influential and seminal film, *Jedda*. I'm not sure why my parents took my sisters and me to see the movie but it certainly left a lasting impression!

In the film, Jedda was an Aboriginal girl who was born on a cattle station in the Northern Territory. After her mother's death, she was raised by the station boss's wife, Sarah McMann. Sarah taught Jedda European ways and separated her from other Aboriginal people.

As Jedda grew into a young woman, she became curious about an Aboriginal man from the bush, named Marbuck. One night, Marbuck lured Jedda to his camp through song and abducted her, and they set off for his tribal land through crocodile-infested swamps.

When Marbuck eventually reached his tribe – with Jedda in tow – the tribal council declared that he had committed a serious crime and as punishment they sang his death song. Driven insane by the song, Marbuch took Jedda to a tall cliff where they both perished. It was a very intense film.

Written, produced and directed by Australian filmmaker Charles Chauvel in 1955, *Jedda* was the first Australian film to star two Aboriginal actors (Robert Tudawali and Ngarla Kunoth) in the leading roles, and also the first Australian feature film shot in colour.

Jedda set a standard for future Australian films. It won more international attention than any previous Australian films, and director Charles Chauvel was nominated for the Golden Palm Award in the 1955 Cannes Film Festival.

Jedda was a groundbreaking film in 1955 that won international attention and set the standard for the Australian film industry.

Courtesy of Umbrella Entertainment

Who remembers the pain of rubbing a hole in the page using the blue ink eraser?

Courtesy of Pelikan

School-day memories!

Yep, that was the story, the blue part would rub out ink.

But the problem was it also made a hole in the paper if you rubbed too long or pressed too hard ... and boy were you in trouble then!!

Don't care to remember how many times I got the cuts for handing up seriously untidy homework after using one of these.

How about you?

A caravan holiday back in the '50s was a very different experience from today.

No mod cons in the caravan back then, just a place to sleep and eat and not much room to do anything else. Entertainment would have to be taken outside and we would run wild, inventing games. I'll always remember the calls and delighted screams of kids being carefree as we chased each other around the caravan parks.

A caravan holiday in the 1950s was not for the faint-hearted. Very few mod cons and not much room inside.

Alamy

SNT 580
SA The Festival State

Most homes had only one phone, which sat on a 'telephone table'. The table usually had a special place for the latest phone book and Yellow Pages.

Pinterest

Our very first telephone used to sit on its very own telephone table in the hallway or passage and was only used, with permission, for local calls and on Sunday nights when there was a cheaper rate, or in emergencies.

Unlike today when everybody, even some children, have their own mobile phones, the phone was used sparingly – if you even had one! Those were the days when you made plans well in advance and stuck to them.

I think we got our first phone at home sometime in the '60s. Before that, if you needed to make a phone call, it was the public phone or asking a neighbour who might have one. In an emergency we could go to the corner shop, which had the phone on.

The phone being fixed in place in the home did not allow much privacy, and there was no multi-tasking while on a call.

Wow, how times have changed!

There was a time when Christmas decorations were hand-made with paper.

I don't remember lavish Christmas decorations while growing up and most years we wouldn't even have had a tree. I can remember the kitchen (we lived mainly in the kitchen back then) was decorated with paper streamers, honeycomb bells and balls and crepe paper cut-outs that would be hung from the ceiling and walls.

In later years we got a tree at Christmas and tinsel but in those early years up until the late '50s, Christmas decorations were an extravagance we did not need.

What memories do you have of your early Christmases?

Before mass-produced Christmas decorations we had decorations made of crepe paper.

Pinterest

Here's a reminder of the days of the 'check-out chicks'.

Check-out chicks have been around since supermarkets first started. They were packing shoppers' bags and 'ringing up the till' long before the modern-day conveniences of barcodes and Eftpos.

Checkouts have certainly come a long way over the years and with the new digital style, there is less and less need for check-out chicks.

'Check-out chick' Elizabeth Adams wins the GSA-NCR Checker (i.e. supermarket check-out) of the Year 1965.

State Library of New South Wales, H2000.52/24

Is it possible that check-out chicks will one day become a thing of the past?

Were you a check-out chick back in the day?

Almost every backyard had one of these back in the day: a rusty 44-gallon drum.

They were used for lots of different things – e.g. as an incinerator when you didn't have the fancy brick one. They were also placed by the water tank overflow to catch some extra water when it rained. And it was handy if you wanted to be outside in winter – just throw in some wood and light it up, an excellent outdoor heater.

And Bill Kelly from Kleinton, Queensland posted a memory: 'As kids back in the late '60s, we would roll an empty 44-gallon drum up to the top of a hill in a grassy paddock. Two of us would climb in and off we would go. No helmets , no anything. With some luck, we are still here!'

The 'good' drinking glasses, like the good crockery and cutlery, only came out on special occasions.

Courtesy of 'Luola' from Etsy

A rusty-looking 44-gallon drum. They were used for lots of things, including as an incinerator for the weekly rubbish burn-off.

Thinkstock, by Getty Images

At our place we had the 'good' drinking glasses that would only be brought out when there were visitors.

Mostly, the kids had to drink out of the old Kraft Vegemite or Lemon Butter glasses and would never dare get out one of the 'good' glasses. And from memory there was a matching jug, also produced only on special occasions.

We also had the 'good' cutlery and crockery, as did most families of the era, some of which was never even used. I recall that my Mum had a tea set (probably Royal Albert or similar) that lived in the china cabinet and was for 'looking at' only. I believe she went to her grave at 86 years of age and never used that tea set.

I wonder whatever became of it.

#9 FACT

On 26 April 1976, the first boatload of refugees fleeing Vietnam sailed into Darwin Harbour, heralding the start of what has become known today as the 'boat people'. The event barely made the news and the 111 Vietnamese people who arrived in 1976 and '77 were quietly resettled in the community. How times have changed.

Mark Mitchell as Con the Fruiterer.

CBS Records

Talking about some of our favourite TV characters, remember Con the Fruiterer?

Played by actor/comedian Mark Mitchell, Con Dickaletus aka 'Con the Fruiterer' was apparently created after Mark was served by two Greek Australian stall holders at Glenferrie Markets in 1984. The character became known nationally from regular spots in *The Comedy Company*, for which he also created the character of Con's wife, Marika.

Con had six daughters, Roula, Toula, Soula, Voula, Foula and Agape. He also has two sons, Nick and Rick.

Con's catchphrases 'coupla days', 'bewdiful' and 'doesn't madda' entered the Australian vernacular and are still used today. Loved Con, I thought he was very funny!

Back in the day, when a large percentage of Australians smoked, this box of matches was a common sight. Not so much these days.

Courtesy of John Eastwood

John Eastwood sent a photo to share: 'Who remembers having a box of these?'

Thanks John. Back in the day, when almost everybody smoked, Redhead matches were quite common and of course the photo of the old box certainly brings into focus how times have changed. There were a couple of brands I can recall – I think the other big seller in matches was Federal, sold mainly in NSW.

And not forgetting Dick Smith, of course, who introduced his own brand called 'Dickheads'.

You gotta hand it to Dick Smith!

Yum! Here's an image to take you back to your childhood. A tin of golden syrup.

Wikipedia describes golden syrup as 'a light treacle and an amber-coloured form of inverted sugar syrup made in the process of refining sugar cane or sugar beet juice into sugar, or by treatment of a sugar solution with acid. It is used in a variety of baking recipes and desserts. It has an appearance similar to honey and is often used as a substitute where honey is unavailable or prohibitively expensive'. It's actually a key ingredient in Anzac buscuits too.

I loved golden syrup when I was a kid, used to have it on my Grandma's pancakes ... and she made the best pancakes ever. None of this pre-packaged pancake mix. Yes, remember those days when cakes and pancakes ingredients weren't pre-packaged?

Golden Syrup on Grandma's pancakes, a marriage made in heaven.

Courtesy of Peters Milk Bar

1980

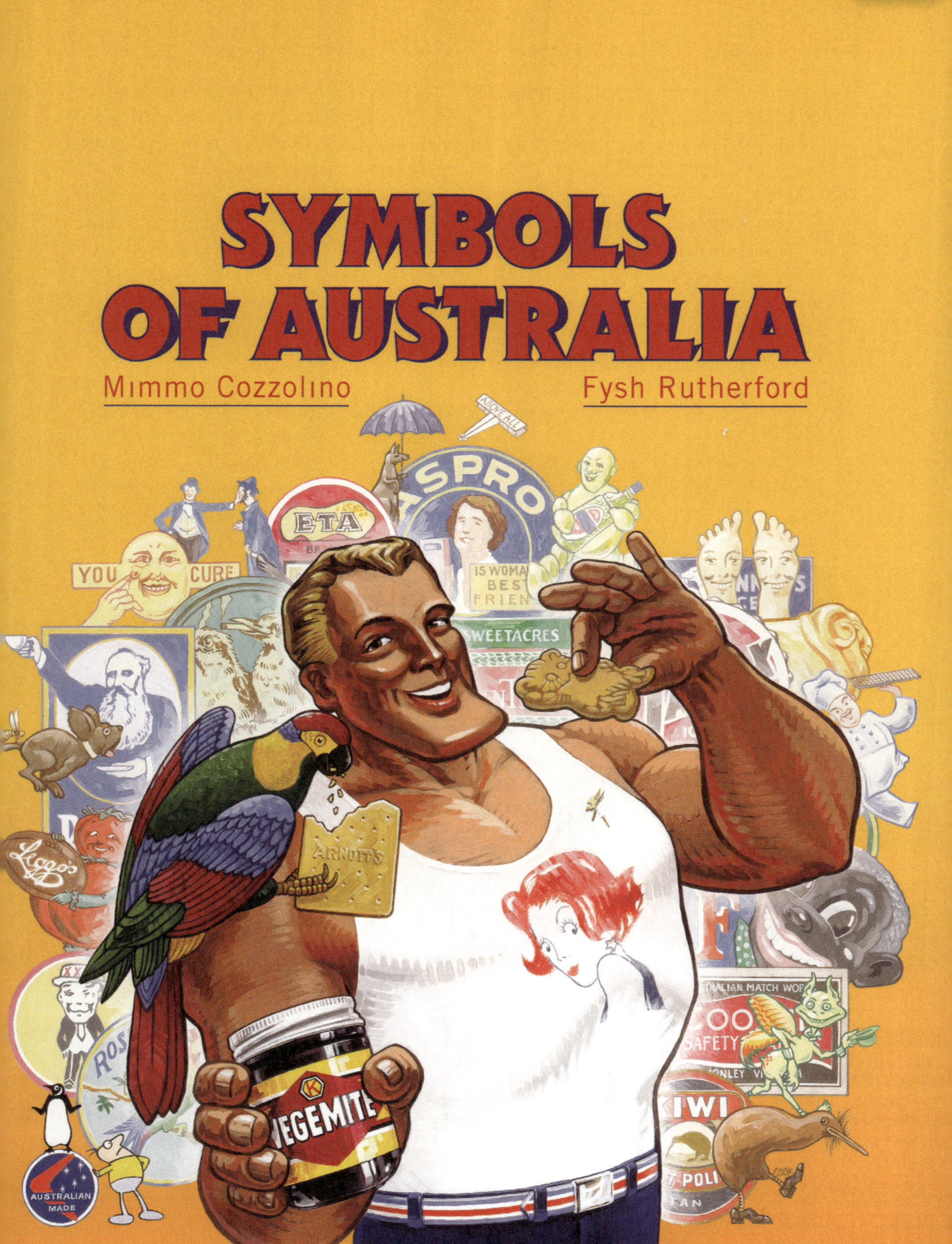

Courtesy of Mimmo Cozzolino

Monie Mat sent me this photo to share: 'Our old family TV'.

Thanks, Monie. Yep, ours was very similar. Vintage 1970s, perhaps when colour TV first came out. No remote control, no VCR or DVD players back then and just the three commercial channels and the ABC.

But, from memory, we loved TV back then. Even though the shows weren't super sophisticated or polished, with very few special effects and no big-name superstars, it was entertainment. Perhaps we'd been starved of it for so long we were prepared to accept just about anything.

Having said that, I feel that some of those old programs would still stand up today ... What do you think?

'There are 4 channels to watch, the picture comes in stunning black and white and it's just a short walk to get up and change the channels!' Imagine the sales pitch back then when TV sets came with no remote, no colour and just Channels 2, 7, 9 and 10. How far has TV come in the last 50 plus years?

I'm talking about the technology rather than programs. I sometimes think there is much less to watch now, even with the almost 20 free-to-air channels, or are we simply harder to please?

Our first TV was a HMV in a wood-grain cabinet with a tuning knob and a volume control and that was about it!

Colour didn't arrive until March 1975. What are your memories of your first TV?

Colour TV was introduced in the mid-70s.

Courtesy of Monie Mat

The first black and white TV sets were manufactured in Australia.

Museums Victoria. Reg. No: MM 125343

PYE
Tecnico
ADMIRAL CANADA
"PHILIPS"

Early model cars were usually fitted out with bench seats in the front. And they were vinyl and used to burn the back of your legs when you sat on them on a really hot day! I can recall that vinyl smell too.

Some of the cars back then had a column gear change up behind the steering wheel so there seemed to be more room in the front of the car. Even the old stick shifts with 'four on the floor' were a lot simpler than today and you could easily fit six people (eight with a bit of a squeeze) in the car.

Seat belts were fitted but not always compulsory back in the day, so more people could pile in the car ... wouldn't be allowed to do it today!

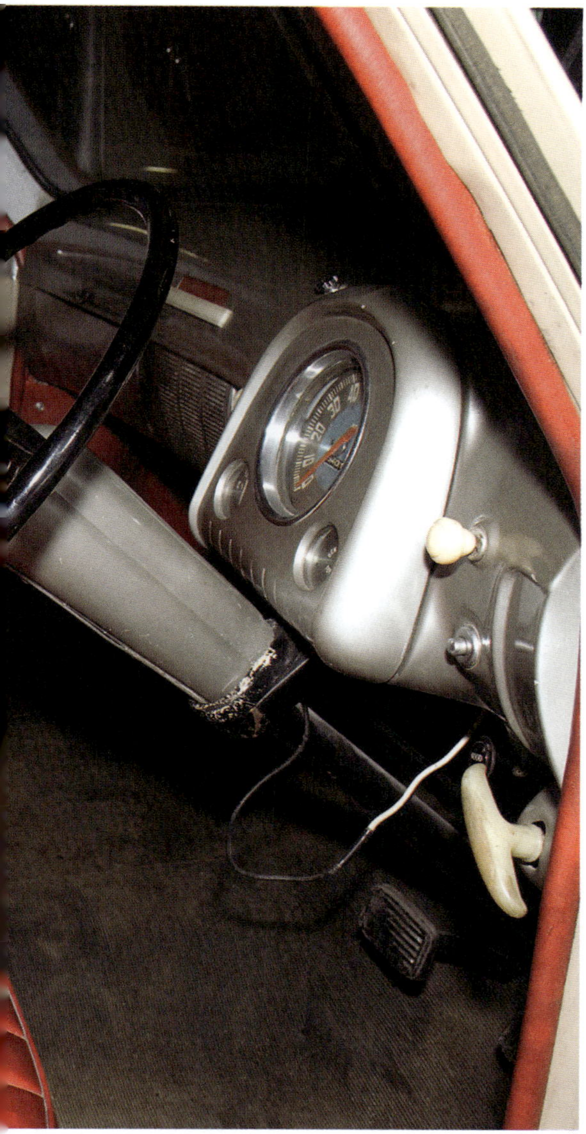

Vinyl front bench seats. Your girlfriend could slide over and sit really close!

Museum of Applied Arts and Sciences, B1662

#10 FACT

Australia's most important collection of vintage motor cycles and cars is housed at the National Motor Museum at Birdwood, about 50 kilometres from Adelaide. The museum contains more than 300 classic vehicles and regularly hosts special events throughout the year. Not just a collection of vehicles, the museum is a social history of how we used to be, the way we are now and the way we will drive into the future.

Holly Hobbie. Memories from the 1970s.

Pinterest

Kay McCaul shared a memory: 'Who remembers Holly Hobbie and the "love is" posters from the 70s?'

The Holly Hobbie craze apparently started in the late 1960s when writer and illustrator Hollie Hobbie (her real name) sold distinctive artwork of a cat-loving, rag-dress-wearing little girl in a giant bonnet to an American greetings card company. This series of illustrations became popular and her originally nameless character became known as Holly Hobbie.

In 1974 somebody came up with the idea of a Holly Hobbie doll that became a huge hit all over the world. It led to a whole range of products and clothing which, as Kay remembers, is a real reminder of the '70s.

Cabbage Patch Kids were all the rage in the early '80s.

I recall the story that they started out as 'The Little People' and were never offered for sale as such but were 'adopted', each coming with their own individual name and birth certificate.

The name change to Cabbage Patch Kids was made in 1982 when toy manufacturer Coleco started to mass-produce the dolls but kept the idea of each doll having a name and birth certificate.

The craze lasted for about three years in Australia, from memory, and I can remember my youngest daughter insisted on taking her two adopted 'children' with us on holiday to New Zealand. I believe she still has her Cabbage Patch dolls to this day.

Cabbage Patch Kids was one of the most popular toy fads of the 1980s.

Courtesy of Cabbage Patch Kids

Birth Cert
and
Adoption Pa
Cabbage Patch Kids
Cabbage Patch Kids™
My friends at the Cabbage Patch™ gave me a name, but if you want to change it when you adopt me, I'll love you just as much!
"I'm one of a kind. I'm Adoptable!"
Ages 3 & up

Pinterest

Bring back the good old brown paper bag.

Shutterstock

What is it with those states (NSW in particular) that are finding it so difficult to live without plastic bags?

In South Australia, single use plastic bags were banned back in 2009 and the world did not end. Australians are using over 5 billion plastic bags every year and many of these ended up in the litter stream. Clean Up Australia volunteers report that 8 per cent of the plastics they remove from our streets, parks, beaches, bushland and waterways are plastic bags. Once these bags enter our environment they are destructive and end up killing many animals that confused them with food. It's a horrible way for poor animals to die, especially when we can easily do without them.

Maybe we could bring back single use paper bags. What do you think?

Professor Julius Sumner Miller was an icon for Cadbury chocolate in the '80s period with his quirky household experiments such as the memorable 'egg-in-the-bottle' experiment! And who would forget his catch phrase ... 'Why is it so?'

The original TV series was broadcast from 1963 to 1986 and became an instant hit known for its 'cool experiments, interesting science, and fantastic hair'. The professor introduced each episode with the line: 'How do you do, ladies and gentlemen, and boys and girls [sometimes adding 'and teachers']. I am Julius Sumner Miller, and physics is my business.'

In the 1980s Julius Sumner Miller appeared in a famous series of Australian television commercials for Cadbury chocolate, using his stock phrase 'Why is it so?', demonstrating a simple scientific principle, and describing how each block of chocolate 'embraces substantial nourishment and enjoyment,' and contained 'a glass and a half of full-cream dairy milk.' The ads were so popular that they continued to be played for some years after his death.

'Each block embraces substantial nourishment and enjoyment and contains a glass and a half of full cream dairy milk'. Professor Julius Sumner Miller

Cadbury

How different to today was your neighbourhood and the neighbours as you were growing up?

The streets of our neighbourhood were filled with children. These were the Baby Boomer years, pre-birth control, and families of four and five children were the norm. We were surrounded by many other young families, all around the same ages, so best friends were always in plentiful supply. The streets and backyards were our territory and our parents never seemed to care where we were or who we were with.

We'd spend hours away from home exploring, riding bikes, playing games, making dams in gutters on rainy days and – at times – getting into fights with the kids from the next street over.

I'm sure there are still great neighbours today but electric roller doors have created a cocooned existence, where a neighbour is no longer seen, let alone spoken to.

How different from our experience growing up with neighbours who were in our lives and almost part of our family.

In the Baby Boomer years we grew up with neighbours' kids all around us. There was always someone to play with.

Source unknown

#11 FACT

The funnel-web spider, one of the most dangerous spiders on Earth, is able to kill a human in 15 minutes. They are found everywhere, except Western Australia and the Northern Territory. Its fangs are powerful enough to bite through gloves and fingernails. In fact, there are at least 40 species of funnel-web spider; not all are dangerous. Funnel-webs hunt mostly at night and normally eat insects but they do lurk in swimming pools in leafy suburbs.

I must admit I was not a good Boy Scout. Growing up as a Boomer child almost everybody spent some time as a Boy Scout or Girl Guide. You'd start out as a Cub or Brownie and get promoted to a Scout or Guide as you got older.

In this photo, we can see members of a newly-formed Fourteenth Canberra Troop of Boy Scouts either at their first camp, or practising for it at an unidentified location near the Murrumbidgee River in the ACT.

There would be a scout camp once a year where we would be taken to a camping ground or out in the bush and have to learn things like making a fire, preparing camping food and boiling water over an open fire. We also made things out of sticks and wood ... bushcraft skills!

At the end of a rather agonising few days you got a badge to sew on your scout's uniform.

I wasn't a very willing Boy Scout. How about you?

Dib, dib, dib, dob, dob, dob. Our parents encouraged us to become Boy Scouts and Girl Guides. It was seen as a great opportunity.

National Archives of Australia, A1200, L24133

Cup, saucer and plate set with the Coles Stores insignia.

Museums Victoria. Reg. No: HT 36288

For several generations of Australians, a visit to Coles Cafeteria was the highlight of a trip to the city.

The first Coles Cafeteria was opened on 21 March 1930, in Melbourne's Bourke Street. It was Australia's first in-store cafeteria and took up an entire floor, with seating for more than 1000 people.

Cafeterias based on the Melbourne model were soon introduced at Coles stores in other capitals and major cities and in the '50s were serving over 20 000 meals per day.

For later generations, the Coles Cafeteria seems to have a strong association with grandmas. The nostalgia factor is significant, with many penning thoughts such as, 'Oh yes I remember Coles cafeteria. The school holiday outing was called "going to town". We dressed in our best clothes including a hat and gloves and after the shopping it was lunch at Coles Cafeteria. The desserts always looked like colourful jewels in their parfait glasses. Especially the jellied fruit, such a treat.'

Sunday was family day and just about everything came to a standstill.

When most Baby Boomers were growing up in post-war Australia, weekend trading was very limited and on Sundays almost everything was closed.

Back then, Sunday was 'a day of rest' and most families from our neighbourhood went to church in the morning and had a hot roast meal for lunch in both winter and summer, followed by a rest in the afternoon before an evening of settling down to listen to the wireless with 'The Lux Theatre' or 'Harry Dearth's Playhouse'.

The Australia of those years seems like something from another planet when compared to today's modern lifestyle of 24/7 'open-for-business' attitude.

I sometimes think our parents and their parents before them knew how to do something we've now totally forgotten ... How to stop!

Everything closed down on Sundays. In some places – like this park in Elsternwick – you weren't even allowed to play in the park.

Source unknown

ELSTERNWICK PARK
COMMITTEE OF MANAGEMENT
PLAYING OF GAMES
IN THIS PARK ON
SUNDAYS IS NOT
ALLOWED

At one time, almost every backyard in Australia had a chook house and it was usually the kids that had the job of feeding the chooks and collecting the eggs.

After-school chores always included taking all the household kitchen scraps and some wheat pellets down to the chooks. Occasionally my father would mix up a special blend of bran and pollard which he would carefully measure out for them and there were times too when he would let the chooks out to scratch around down the bottom of the yard.

Collecting the eggs was pretty important because woe betide you if you happened to drop an egg and break it. We always had a supply of fresh eggs and they were also used in neighbourhood bartering as well.

With smaller backyards and busy schedules, very few families keep chooks anymore. Did you have a chook house in your backyard growing up?

Before-school chores included feeding the chooks and collecting the eggs.

Alamy

We were forbidden to play down at the creek but sometimes the temptation was just too much.

State Library Victoria, H2015.198/54b

The greatest advantage of being a child growing up in the Boomer years was the freedom!

It was always strictly forbidden to play down at the creek but on a really hot weekend we could never resist the lure of the water.

To get to it you had to go through the bush where there were ticks and there were leeches in the creek itself.

In the winter it could run really fast but in summer it was just a pool, sometimes a bit stagnant and smelly, but it was still water!

At times our adventures needed extra equipment, like jars and nets made from old stockings. These were used to catch frogs or taddies (tadpoles). We needed to be very strategic about where we were going to catch them and much planning went into these 'sorties'. There were several spots along the creek designated as the 'best spots' and so we would often split up, comparing our catch when we met up later in the day.

At other times, we could make a spontaneous decision to head further upstream where there was usually deeper water and we'd go 'skinny-dipping'. Completely without any adult supervision, we would swim and play in the water for hours.

Mum would say, 'You haven't been swimming in that creek again have you?' We'd shake our heads, forgetting of course that our hair and clothes were still damp.

Just reminiscing on some of the games we all played at school and the equipment that we used to play on: much of it now would be considered unsafe, of course. I got thinking about the monkey bars that came in a number of different shapes and styles, including the big one that was a real challenge to any kid.

It was a good climb to the top of this one and a long way down if you happened to lose your grip, and you'd hit ten bars on the way down before you landed on the concrete below. So you learned to hang on!!

I look at this photo now and I certainly wouldn't be game enough to climb this, but I remember climbing one of these when I was a kid. Can you?

Now considered too dangerous, monkey bars were popular in the school playground.

Pinterest

Our Friday night special desert was a brick of ice cream. My favourite was chocolate or Neapolitan.

Courtesy of Ephemera Society/Photo by Mimmo Cozzolino

Before we had tubs of ice cream we used to buy a brick. When fridges were first introduced they had a small rectangular freezer inside the fridge itself which was only big enough to hold an ice block tray and not much else. The ice-cream manufacturers came up with the rectangular brick of ice cream, which was just the right size to fit into the freezer.

On Friday night, Mum's only night off from cooking the family meal, we'd have takeaway fish and chips with lots of salt and vinegar and then Dad would carefully divide the brick of ice cream into six very equal portions which we'd have with Mum's home-made preserved peaches ... Ah, sweet memories!

#12

FACT

As Jan O'Connell writes in her fascinating book, *A Timeline of Australian Food*, spaghetti bolognese is Australia's third-most preferred dish, after steak and roast chicken. The first recipe for spag bol appeared in the *Australian Women's Weekly* in July 1952 as part of a feature on party suppers. It advised baking it and including Worcestershire sauce, two things no-one would dream of doing now.

Every playground had one of these!

Pinterest

On a hot summer's day, you'd end up with second-degree burns on the back of your legs and your bum after sliding down one of these.

Every playground had one of these very basic slippery dips, with the ladder up to the top, and when you'd climbed all the way up, there was only one way down!

I can remember at school we had 15 steps to the top and there would be a kid on every rung waiting for their turn to go hurtling to the bottom.

They still have slippery dips in playgrounds but I notice there's a bit more protection both on the ladder and on the sides of the slide and cushioning material at the bottom.

To get a 'carbon copy', you had to physically place a piece of carbon paper between two A4 sheets of paper before winding them into the typewriter.

These days with technology there's no need for such things as 'carbon copies' ... just save the document in 'Word' and you can print off as many times as you like. And remember the little bottle of 'White-Out'? Fine for the original document (well, sort of) but then you had to correct the carbon copy, and that was a whole different story.

How on earth did we survive without computers? Can anyone remember?

When the words 'carbon copy' really meant a carbon copy.

Courtesy of 'This is not a Job for Superheroes' blog

It's difficult to imagine in this digital age, just how huge the photographic industry really was.

In Australia Kodak distributed a wide range of products, such as cameras, film, paper and chemicals. Photographers – both amateur and professional – as well as medical and graphic artists used their products.

Founded by George Eastman in 1888, Kodak filed for bankruptcy in February 2012, a victim of the digital technology age.

Who remembers picking up the photos from the chemist shop in one of these Kodak wallets, photos on one side and negatives on the other?

Your developed photos would be presented in a Kodak envelope, photos on one side and negatives on the other side.

Museums Victoria. Reg. No: HT 23164

String art was a craze that swept through Australia in the 1970s.

Courtesy of Etsy, Merakii9 (instagram.com/amitaanne/)

String art was all the rage back in the 1970s. String art uses coloured string, wool or wire to create geometric patterns. The 'string' is normally held between nails hammered into a base board. Multiple straight lines of string can form shapes ranging from simple curves to more complex designs resembling flowers, sailing boats, etc.

The popularity of string art kits reached its peak in the 1970s when numerous households had a homemade string art picture on the wall.

We still have a few of these somewhere out in the garage, don't know why we haven't thrown them out yet.

Do you still have some string art from the '70s?

Something many of us reared in the 1950s will immediately identify, a smoker's table complete with ash tray.

Courtesy of Ian Keith Kershaw

Ian Keith Kershaw shared a photo and some memories of years gone by:

> Anyone brought up in the 1950s would remember the smoker stand tables that were common in many homes. The ashtray could swing around the table and it had a holder that would take an open box of matches. Very smelly when left overnight un-emptied. Don't miss these things one little bit!

Amazing to think that it wasn't all that many years ago that smoking in public places was simply accepted as the norm. In restaurants, workplaces, lifts, airplanes, indoor sporting arenas smokers could just light up and nobody ever complained very much. Imagine what would happen today if you lit up in a public place? It's a very different world!

Here's another great Australian invention, the Esky.

First introduced back in 1952, the term 'Esky' is also commonly used in Australia to generically refer to portable coolers or ice boxes and is part of the Australian vernacular, in place of words like 'cooler' or 'cooler box' and the New Zealand 'chilly bin'.

The Esky was created by Malley's, a Sydney refrigeration business. Some historians have credited Malley's with the invention of the portable ice cooler. According to the company, the Esky, was 'recognised as the first official portable cooler in the world'.

According to Malley's, 500 000 Australian households owned one (in a country of approximately ten million) by 1960. Remember your first Esky?

The 'Esky' has become an essential item in every Australian household.

Courtesy of Scrapdogs on eBay

Remember drinking water straight from the hose?

Museums Victoria. Reg. No: MM 010420

From the *Daily Mail*:

Congratulations to all my friends who were born in the 1940s, 50s and 60s.

First, we survived being born to mothers who smoked and/or drank sherry while they carried us and lived in houses made of asbestos.

They took aspirin, ate blue cheese, bread and dripping, raw egg products, loads of bacon and processed meat, and didn't get tested for diabetes or cervical cancer.

Then, after that trauma, our baby cots were covered with bright coloured lead-based paints. We had no childproof lids on medicine bottles, and when we rode our bikes, we had no helmets or shoes.

As children, we would ride in cars with no seatbelts or air bags.

We built treehouses and dens and played in riverbeds with Matchbox cars.

We had friends and we went outside and found them!

We fell out of trees, got cut, broke bones and teeth and there were no lawsuits from these accidents. And we ate worms and mud pies made from dirt and we drank water from the garden hose, not from a bottle.

David Mason sent a photo of the electric jug made by Speedie: 'Used it this morning for morning tea. Plus I've got a brown one with a cut off feature. My folks and my late grandparents used them all the time and we had some in various sizes. It even uses the same cord as the toaster too. I saved this one from going to the dump.'

David reckons you can still get the replacement elements too. I'm thinking when my latest electric kettle gives up the ghost I'll be off to the secondhand shop to look for one of these. With a couple of spare elements it would probably last a lot longer than a brand new electric kettle from Harvey Normans and at a quarter the price ... even less.

An original electric jug. You could repair these by replacing the element. No electrician needed!

Courtesy of David Mason

Regular reader Judy Chappell commented that she recalls her mother's cooking was done with wood: 'My mother even made bread in the wood stove and her stews would simmer for hours on the back of the stove.'

Thanks, Judy. I still remember my mum's Irish stew! It must have been a real art to produce some of the dishes our mothers and grandmothers were able to serve up without such modern amenities as gas or fan-forced ovens and temperature control.

Imagine trying to bake without a temperature gauge? That is what most of our mothers did. They controlled the temperature by burning the right amount of wood to ash then testing it by sticking their hands in. Adding more wood for heat or leaving the door open to cool. Simple enough. Though they ran the risk of burning their hands.

I seem to recall that our first electric stove arrived sometime in the 1960s, which meant no more chopping wood, more concise temperature control and a cleaner kitchen without the old wood box near the stove.

What do you remember about your mum's cooking?

Before electric and gas ovens all the cooking was done in or on a wood stove.

State Library Victoria, H2009.88/129

1940s

Cathy Tallent shared a photo and some memories: 'Remember the old Commonsense cookbook? This was my mother's, reprinted 1956. It's still in use, although I have to substitute a few ingredients.'

The Commonsense Cookery Book was compiled by the NSW Public School Cookery Teachers' Association and, according to Booktopia, 'is a kitchen classic which has been teaching people kitchen basics for nearly a century.

First published in 1914, and with one million copies sold, this is the book every home leaver takes with them when they fly the nest. It contains recipes for everything from how to make toast to more complex dishes.'

The Commonsense Cookery Book, 1956.

Courtesy of Cathy Tallent

Paul Stempel posted a comment sure to stir your memory: 'My wife pulled out her nearly ancient copy of Margaret Fulton's cookbook last night to find a recipe she hadn't used in more than two decades. She wanted to make an Orange Cake recipe from the book.'

Margaret Fulton's first cookbook came out in 1968 and she is credited with being the first food writer to encourage the Australian housewives of the day to think past the meat and three veg meals.

Do you still have, and maybe even still use, her famous cookbook?

The Margaret Fulton Cook Book, first published in 1968, has sold one and a half million copies.

Courtesy of Hardie Grant Publishing

MARGARET FULTON COOKBOOK
QUALITY & VALUE
SUMMIT
FROM THE PAUL HAMLYN GROUP

1957

Judie Munro shared a memory about her childhood:

> Monday was wash day, Tuesday was ironing day, Wednesday was mending, sewing, and baking day, Thursday was cleaning day, Friday was shopping day, Saturday was for sports and Sunday was for Worship and Church and after Church while still in good clothes, visiting rellies and friends, and tea at one of the Nanas on Sunday night.

Thanks, Judie, that was just about it at our place too, except Sunday was a big roast lunch at home. Sunday afternoon was a 'doss' down for Mum (afternoon nap).

After tea, all sitting around the wireless listening to 'Harry Dearth's Playhouse', then a wash, then bed. Sounds terribly boring, but thinking back, it was very comforting to have that kind of routine in a young life.

And Monday was most definitely washday. The wood was cut and stacked so the copper could be lit and brought to the boil nice and early. Clothes would be on the line by lunchtime.

After they came off the line the clothes were 'damped down' in preparation for ironing the following day. What hard work!

I still have a strong memory of my dear Mum with her big basket of clothes, standing at the ironing board for hours and listening to the serials on the wireless as she did the damping down.

Tuesday was ironing day.

State Library Victoria, H84.201/14

#13

FACT

It's the Australian invention credited with increasing consumption of wine worldwide. It was also preferred by producers of less expensive wines as it is cheaper than glass bottles. Known by various and often unflattering names – 'chateau cardboard', 'goon bag' and 'bag in a box' – the humble wine cask was the brainchild of South Australian winemaker Tom Angove. He first patented the design in 1965.

Now here's a blast from the past.

In the 1970s we used to have fondue dinner parties. There'd be four to six people sitting around a table in kaftans, dipping bread into a warm bowl of melted cheese or dipping chunks of beef into a pot of bubbling oil.

In either case, much cask wine was consumed and many opinions were espoused as Neil Diamond's 'Hot August Night' played on the radiogram. The meals were simple to prepare and clean-up was easy.

Back then, judging by how many newlyweds received multiple fondue pots as wedding gifts, people must have thought of fondue as the ideal meal for people with limited cooking ability. At the end of the main meal, it was a different fondue pot, this time with melted chocolate with dipping pieces of fruit or marshmallows.

The 1970 fondue dinner party with cheap wine. The dessert was usually melted chocolate and pieces of fruit.

Wikipedia, photo Christophe Clement

'Hot August Night', released in 1972, sold over two million copies in Australia.

Courtesy of MCA Records Australia

Those who were there in the '70s will remember there was one artist who appeared in almost every suburban record collection around the nation and whose songs could be heard at just about every backyard barbie and neighbourhood party.

Neil Diamond's 'Hot August Night' spend almost 30 weeks at number one in the Aussie charts, and he did a triumphant tour all around Australia in 1976, ending in a massive farewell concert that was filmed and broadcast on television.

That show broke attendance records at the Sydney Sports Ground and Neil Diamond cemented his place as one of Australia's favourite pop music stars.

At any 1970s dinner party, complete with a fondue and cheap wine, Neil Diamond could almost always be heard on the radiogram.

Have you still got your copy of 'Hot August Night'?

Every year we sat for the final end-of-year exam at school.

There was a time when students were required to pass a written test at the end of each school year. To progress to the next grade, both in primary and secondary school, every student had to pass the test, otherwise they were kept back.

And they really were kept back!

Exams were always pretty scary, usually held in the classroom and it was almost always stinking hot! I was a fairly average student but managed to get through exams – never a great or top ten result, I generally finished somewhere in the first twenty.

Kids these days don't have to face the big end-of-year exams like we used to. How did you go with the annual test?

At the end of each school year there would be an exam. If you failed that exam you were kept back to repeat the year again.

State Library of Queensland, 71776

On the subject of school days ... There was a time when school teachers taught at the same school for their entire careers.

This is my mother-in-law, Dorothy Chamberlain, who taught Grade 2 at the same school from 1955 to 1981, 24 years of her life as a devoted teacher.

Back then, teachers were always addressed as 'Sir' or 'Miss' (or 'Mrs'), always dressed in a suit and tie or skirt and were usually very strict disciplinarians.

Who was your favourite teacher at school and why? Do you remember a teacher you hated?

My mother-in-law, Dorothy Chamberlain, taught the same class at the same school for 26 years.

Bob Byrne

#14 FACT

Prior to 1954 there were no black boxes, no cockpit voice recorders nor flight data recorders. It wasn't until several high-profile crashes of de Havilland Comet airliners went unsolved that Australian researcher David Warren invented the black box flight recorder to record cockpit noise and instruments during flight. His invention has made a huge contribution to international aviation safety.

Part of Australian folklore, the Royal Flying Doctor Service, started by Reverend John Flynn as the Aerial Medical Service in 1928.

Wikipedia, photo CT Bolt

Robert Sanchez from ReliveDigital sent a photo: 'Just ask anyone in Australia's remote communities what they think of the men and women of the Royal Flying Doctor Service and you'll quickly realise what a lifeline they provide.'

Have you or your family ever needed them?

Australian coins before 1966 and decimal currency.

Courtesy of Ian Keith Kershaw

I managed to keep some pre-decimal coins. I'm glad I kept a few in my collection as they bring back memories of coins in Christmas puddings or using them at penny arcades.

Slang terms for these were:

Halfpennys were also called 'hape-neys'

Threepence: throopence, tray or trey

Sixpence: zac, zack or tanner

Shilling: bob or deener or dina

Two shilling/Florin: two bob or sly.

There was also the farthing, which I think might have been discontinued in the late '40s, and back in the '30s there was a gold sovereign.

Some pre-decimal coins have become very valuable. According to the Wynyard Coin Centre, if you have a 1930 penny, it could fetch you over $40 000 on the collectors' market.

Other valuable coins include a 1955 halfpenny and penny pair (over $17 000) and a 1923 halfpenny valued at $1000.

The Royal Australian Mint has recently started to sell threepences and sixpences in a coin pack so they can be used in the Christmas pudding, which was the tradition during the Baby Boomer years.

Who remembers their first pedal car?

Museums Victoria. Reg. No: MM 8623

Your first Cyclops pedal car was a special toy indeed. I had a red one, which I drove around the backyard as a kid and I still remember how I'd pretend to be the bus driver dropping other kids off after school.

Such is the imagination of a six- or seven-year-old.

I recall my pedal car had a tray on the back and at other times I would be driving a truck with a big load of dirt. Pushed that pedal car around the yard for hours and let my imagination run wild. I would love to think children still do that sort of thing today even though they have much more creative toys and many more of them!

Were all kids really that skinny in the '50s? This black and white photo from the Museums Victoria collection shows six boys playing a game of marbles. It was taken in Perth, Western Australia in April 1955 in a government school.

In the '50s and '60s children mainly played outdoors and joined in some very vigorous games. I wonder if we were this skinny though.

Does anyone remember the kind of games they played at school during breaks?

Kids in Australia in the '50s played some very energetic games, and were almost always outdoors.

Museums Victoria. Reg. No: MM 104112

It wasn't all that unusual for boys to have a fight in the schoolyard.

Alamy

When I was at school in the '50s and '60s there were often fights in the schoolyard, usually up behind the shelter sheds where the teachers couldn't see what was going on.

The fights were usually about playground supremacy; these days it would be considered bullying. There was always a bully at school but somehow we managed to survive.

I was bullied at school in about Grade 3 and told my father. His advice: 'Stand up to a bully and he'll back away'. I eventually did stand up for myself, and the bully and I later became good friends.

Were you ever bullied at school?

Shintaro from the *The Samurai* TV series – after-school TV in the 1960s.

Turner Entertainment

Joseph Russo shared this photo of Shintaro from *The Samurai* series which was shown on TV in the '60s: 'Every kid's favourite TV show.'

Lots of my friends loved this show when we were at school in the 1960s. It was massive in Australia and when Koichi Ose toured in 1965, he was mobbed just like the Beatles.

I remember the series well, and the fact that it was badly dubbed made it even more entertaining. Tombay the Mist and Shintaro did a wonderful job keeping Japan a safe and honest place. Their backward leaps into the trees and star weapons were the stuff of science fiction but kids loved the show. Hillarious, really.

Lisa Stevens sent in a photo: 'Does anyone remember the big weighing scales that you put money in to read your weight, similar to this?'

Thanks, Lisa, and what about the talking scales that spoke your weight, probably not thought of as all that extraordinary these days, but back in the '50s/'60s I was always fascinated by them. We had a talking set of scales at the Adelaide Railway Station and whenever I went into the city by train I would always marvel at the 'talking scales'.

I also remember these big scales, usually outside the chemist shop. For 1d (one penny) you could get your accurate weight printed out on a little card.

For a penny these scales would tell your weight. We all thought that was amazing!

Courtesy of Lisa Stevens

There wasn't much in the way of fashion for kids when we were growing up in a post-war Australia.

The average kid's wardrobe was mainly homemade clothes and hand-me-downs. There were three sets – play clothes, school clothes and Sunday best for 'going out'.

I remember a lot of grey serge short pants made by Stamina; my sisters' dresses were mostly made by Mum or Grandma.

Underclothes were terrible. Boys wore Chesty Bonds singlets and Y-fronts while my sisters wore poplin bloomers that went grey and baggy!

The girls had good Sunday dresses but for boys it was more of the same ... grey suit with a clean white shirt and tie.

What are some memories of the way we were dressed back in the day?

Sunday best for little girls in the 1940s.

Courtesy of Bestway Knitwear

BESTWAY
KNITWEAR
A2468
4D.
4, 6 and 8 YEARS
2, 2½ or 3 ozs. of 2-ply

Reader Kenny Peplow shared this old Kodak slide that took me back to the days when we would head off on a motoring holiday as a family.

No air conditioning, no dual carriageway, no passing lanes, no seatbelts. What an adventure. How did the kids cope back then?

Dad smoked in the car and listened to the races or the footy. And if it was hot the only air con was winding down all the windows to let in the hot air. And if it was freezing, Dad would wind down the window to knock the ash of his cigarette.

There was always a water bag in the front of the car and every so often we would stop for a drink of water served in anodised beakers. No soft drinks.

There were lots of bickering between siblings about who was taking up too much space and inevitably all the kids joined in the chorus, 'Are we there yet? ... Are we there yet?'

So much has changed now with the family touring holiday. Cars are bigger, more comfortable and fitted with all the latest safety equipment, seat belts for all, air conditioning and some even have individual DVD screens for the children in the back seats. There are also iPads and iPhones, tablets or hand held mini-computers on which to watch movies, play games and listen to music.

But what terrific memories I now have of those family car trips. How about you?

Family trips were always a great adventure but with none of the modern conveniences that kids have today.

Courtesy of Kenny Peplow

There were regular health check-ups in school by a visiting doctor or nurse.

Courtesy of Community History South Australia

We had regular health check-ups at school. The various education departments around the country introduced health checks, including dental checks. It was a bit like the school milk program: it might have seemed a good idea at the time but most kids hated it!

Most children were pretty healthy. In fact, it was a rare (and very embarrassing) thing to be sick or get hurt in the playground, and if somebody vomited that was even worse. From memory there was a bucket of sawdust kept under the stairs at school and if somebody threw up, someone was ordered to throw the sawdust over it.

And what about the sick bay, always had that disinfectant smell!

#15 FACT

Who can forget Cathy Freeman's glorious win at the 2000 Sydney Olympics? Synonymous with Australian Olympic glory, Cathy is a former 400-metre sprinter who at the age of just 16 became the first Indigenous Australian to win Commonwealth gold. And at the 2000 Sydney Olympics she became only the second Australian Aboriginal to claim gold. She retired from athletics in 2003.

Mello Yello was one of those drinks that Coca-Cola released in the late '70s, I believe.

It was a very highly caffeinated, citrus-flavored soft drink and was actually introduced to compete with Pepsi's Mountain Dew.

Mello Yello was withdrawn from Australia in the early 1990s and replaced with the similar but uncaffeinated Lift.

This photo is of a Mello Yello Russell yo-yo which is now a real collector's item and sells for up to $50 or more on eBay.

I've still got a few red Coca-Cola yo-yos. Sadly, though, they're the most common and not worth very much.

Mello Yellow was a citrus flavoured soft drink from the Coca-Cola company.

Courtesy of Owen Webster

When I was a boy growing up, at about seven years old, Father Christmas left me a Meccano set for Christmas.

Meccano was our equivalent to Lego. All the parts were steel and had to be joined by little nuts and bolts and the set came complete with a little tool kit of a small screwdriver and spanners.

There were varying size kits with steel plates, strips, wheels, axles and all manner of models could be made. I spent many hours building all sorts of model trucks, cranes and buildings.

Fairly basic when compared to the toys of today but I'm sure there are many of us from that era that will recall the fun they had with their Meccano set.

A popular toy for boys in the 1950s, a Meccano set.

eBay

An important part of our education from the 1970s, the ABC's *Everybody Sing!*.

Courtesy of the ABC

Lindsay MacAgue sent a photo with the comment: 'How I wish they still had these in primary school.'

The ABC's 'Everybody Sing!' program, which started on-air in 1975, finished in 2014.

Everybody Sing! had been a valued resource kit for music education in many Australian primary schools. It was produced by a team of music education specialists and the annual song book and teachers' handbook, along with the radio program and, later, CDs, provided teachers with a complete set of resources to get kids singing, tapping to the beat and understanding the fundamentals of music.

At the end of the 2014 program the ABC announced there would be no program published in 2015 as 'work is underway to devise a new Sing! program that fulfils the requirements of the modern classroom.'

Kevin Banister shared some memories:

Growing up as a kid in the late '50s, early '60s, breakfast was porridge, vegemite on toast or weetbix, but, there was always something, for me and my brothers.

Warm milk in a small bottle at school and ordered your lunch from the 'tuck' shop with your name and class written on a brown paper bag and money enclosed. (St. Josephs, Rozelle). Rode your bike or scooter on the street without a helmet, without having to dodge the cars. Played street cricket where the light/telegraph pole was the wicket and hitting the ball onto a roof was 6 and out. When the street lights came on it was time to go home.

Played in the rain and mud and made mud pies in your back yard or down at the park. Where playing 'on line' meant swinging on the Hills Hoist using it as a merry-go-round. Played on the slippery dip, swings, merry-go-round, monkey bars at the park and came back with some bumps, bruises and cuts and mum would kiss it better and bung on a band aid.

'We came back from play with bumps, bruises and cuts and Mum would kiss it better and bung on a band aid.'

iStock

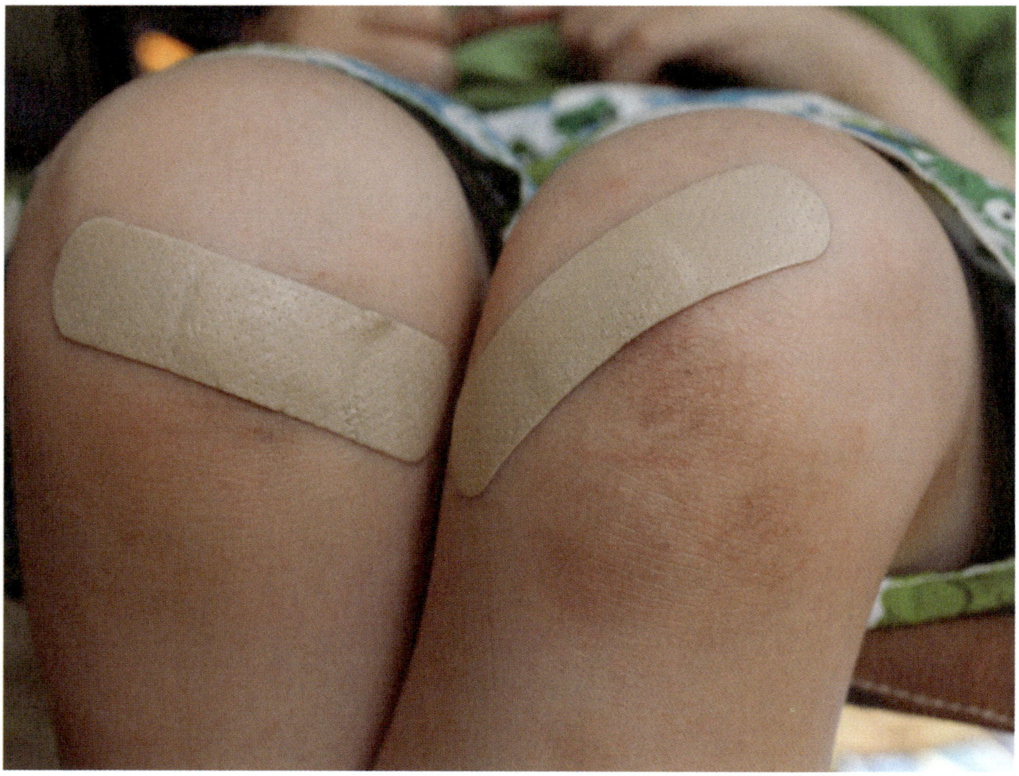

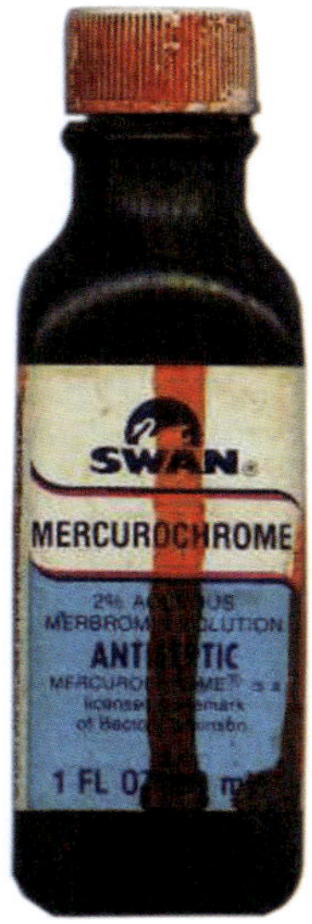

'This is going to sting!' Mercurochrome was part of the home remedy chest.

8tracks.com

Just thinking about some of the home remedies we used to have in the medicine chest at home when we were kids.

Back then, a trip to the doctor was a pretty rare event. Most of the cuts and abrasions, splinters, minor injuries, bruises and nasty bumps were treated by Mum or Grandma with trusted remedies handed down over several generations.

I remember iodine or Mercurochrome for cuts and gashes, Bates Salve for splinters, a poultice or Vicks VapoRub for a wheezy chest and Rawleigh's liniment for bad knocks and bruises.

Then there were home treatments for everything ranging from Laxettes or castor oil for constipation to gargling for a sore throat and a mustard plaster for inflammation.

Strangely, we survived both the ailment and the home remedy! What are some of your memories of home cures?

Grahame Andrews posted some memories of growing up: 'Saturday night was bath night and Mum would put a big dollop of Dettol in the bath to kill the germs. Just as well because I was the third of three boys and by the time I got in the water was brown. Didn't seem to hurt me though ... Good old Dettol.'

Thanks, Grahame. Remember when you'd have a buster off the bike and end up with gravel rash and Mum would bathe it in Dettol? Jeez that was torture!!

The other one I remember was Mercurochrome, which gave you red knees and became something of a badge of honour.

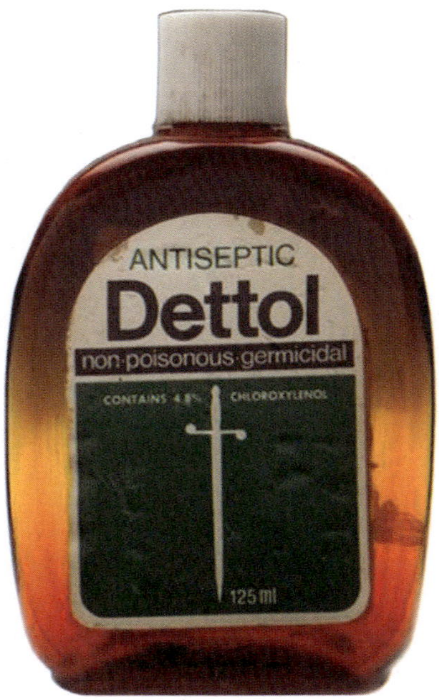

'We always had a big dollop of Dettol in the bath.'

Museums Victoria. Reg. No: SH 912691.11

Be honest now, who gave Dad a bottle of Old Spice aftershave at Christmas?

If I close my eyes I can still see the bottle and box and I can smell it too. Some wonderful memories of Dad, maybe pretending to be really excited with his gift ... and maybe he really was.

Originally marketed with a nautical theme, Old Spice started out as shaving soap and aftershave lotion. It has recently enjoyed a resurgence with a whole new generation after a very successful advertising campaign. The range was expanded to include skin care, antiperspirant and deodorant.

Incidentally, this 1962 bottle and box are going for AUD$40 on eBay at the moment.

Old Spice has enjoyed something of a revival in more recent times and was always Dad's favourite aftershave.

eBay

Ugly Dave Gray, a well-known face on television last century.

Photo by News Ltd/Newspix

Ugly Dave Gray (whose real name is Graham David Taylor), is probably best known as a regular panellist on Graham Kennedy's *Blankety Blanks* in the late 1970s. Before that, in 1976, he played a dramatic role in the early episodes of the soap opera *The Young Doctors*. After his initial 13-week contract expired he left *The Young Doctors* to work on *Blankety Blanks*. Graham Kennedy himself had convinced Gray to do *Blankety Blanks*, and despite taking a pay cut Gray did the show.

In 1973, he hosted an Australian version of the American game show *Beat the Clock* called *Free for All* and in 1977 was appointed Court Jester to King of Moomba Mickey Mouse.

In the 1980s Gray also presented a drive-time radio program on 3UZ, with Mary Hardy.

Ugly Dave Gray is now living in retirement and in 2011 announced that he wished to be cryogenically frozen after his death.

#16 FACT

Australia's first police force was made up entirely of convicts! In 1789 Sydney Town's best behaved convicts were put in charge of guarding the new settlement and were known as the Night Watch. There was no other choice, with little other manpower available. The 12 convicts were organised into four groups to patrol different areas of the settlement.

It seems almost funny today but they were apparently very effective.

Pinterest

Who remembers when some police forces around Australia used Morris Minis to get around?

The Mini was such a popular little car back in the '60s and early '70s that even the police took to using them. However flashing lights, sirens, two-way radios, aerials and police insignia had to be added by the police in each state.

I bought my first (and only) Mini in 1966. Being 6' 2" (in the old measurement), I still wonder how the hell I got into and out of it!

1958

The local repairman was a 'jack-of-all-trades' and could fix or repair almost anything.

Alamy

We had a local repairman who could fix everything from a wireless to a washing machine and just about everything in between.

Sadly we have become such a 'throwaway' society. I recall my Dad putting a new filament in the electric jug and toaster and doing other odd-job repairs at home.

The local repairman was there though when anything electrical broke down – the telly, the wireless, the washing machine – you'd just drop it off to him and in a few days he would have it fixed and back as good as new. These days it seems just as cheap to throw the broken one away and buy a new one.

The old wireless had all the different stations printed by name and they were also segmented into the different states.

The city stations were all highlighted while provincial and country stations were displayed less prominently. These days people tune in to a number on the radio dial, AM, FM or digital and radio stations now have groovy names like 'Hit FM', 'Smooth', 'Mix', etc. Back in the day, all the stations were identified with a number which related to the state of Australia in which they were broadcasting, 2 for New South Wales, 3 for Victoria, 4 for Queensland and so on.

I remember listening to the wireless as a kid, listening to an interstate radio station, which you could only pick up at night, and trying to imagine the people in that far away city or country town. I loved the wireless when I was a child and ended up working in the radio industry for 40 years.

The name of every radio station around Australia was on the wireless dial.

Bob Byrne

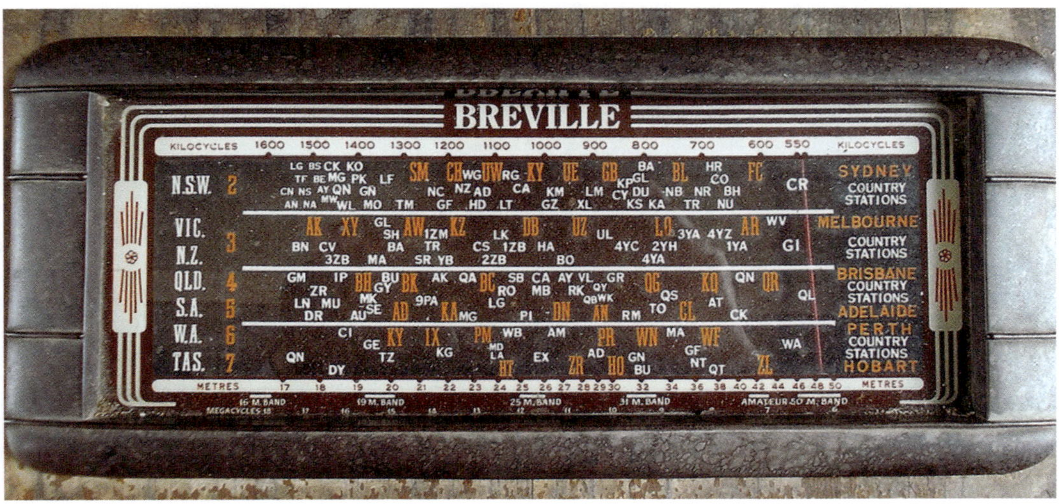

These were on a lot of children's birthday and Christmas 'wish lists' way back last century – 'A box of 72 Derwent pencils, pleeease Mum 'n' Dad!'

Oh my goodness – the joy of receiving a box of them! and sliding up and off the big cardboard boxed lid, to then be able to swing open the two sides that each held 36 pencils and see the wonderful array of 72 creamy soft coloured pencils, all beautifully arranged in three tiers of 12 pencils each, and carefully colour coded.

They were the bee's knees of coloured pencils!

This is the best pic I could find – just wish there was one of a brand new boxed set, but I guess those pencils were all just too tempting not to use, so such a pic doesn't exist!

The jade green and dark crimson pencils were the first ones to wear right down in my set. They were used so often and sharpened so far down that they couldn't be sharpened anymore!

How many times did you almost chip your teeth as a child on one of these?

The old school bubblers were pretty important in schoolyards way back then. We'd never heard of bottled water of course and indeed you would have been laughed at if you had walked around at school with a bottle. I did chip a tooth on a small glass bottle once when we were forced to drink milk at recess time.

My Mum was always concerned about the bubblers though.

The 'bee's knees' of all coloured pencils sets, the derwent complete set.

Etsy

Before the age of plastic water bottles, you got a drink of water from the 'bubbler'.

© Henry Grant Collection/Museum of London

Shane Blackham posted some childhood memories to share:

> When I was a kid in the '70s and '80s we had a playground across the road. It had a steel slide to shoot rockets up, ride your bike down or slide down with soapy water on a hot day. Many bums were burnt when the water dried too quickly.
>
> The steel maypole was great fun except for the egg you got when a ring hit you on the head. The swing was a plank attached at both ends, too often swung dangerously, resulting in broken arms and a broken swing. Had my first kiss on that swing.
>
> The seesaw had its share of sore bums and kisses too. We would nail Catherine Wheels to the fence and watch them spin and flash, and play rounders and later 'murder in the dark'. Made stink bombs from the seed pods on a mysterious tree (crushed with spit), and drew on the footpath with stones.
>
> We made grass forts when the grass was mowed, and fought with wooden swords. In more peaceful times simply watched the bees and looked into the sky to imagine shapes in the clouds. I always thought rainbows were bridges for angels. I was a dreamer. I still am. Thanks for reading my memories.

Thanks for sharing them Shane.

The maypole was always great fun!

Pinterest

When did you first get a mobile phone? Mobiles came out in the very early '80s in Australia. The first call was made on the country's first mobile network – Telecom's new Public Automatic Telephone System.

The very first mobiles cost about $5000 – a fortune at the time. We all thought these new mobile phones were amazing even though they weighed in at a pretty heavy 14 kilograms and could only store 20 numbers in the memory. And you couldn't even send a text message! A text what?

Of course, mobile phones have come a long way since then and when we look at these old dinosaurs now it's a little funny but they were the beginning of the smartphone technology we see today.

Can you remember your first encounter with a mobile phone?

The earliest mobile phones were the size of a house brick but gradually they began to shrink.

Wikipedia

#17 FACT

It wasn't until 1994 that Australians had their very first access to the 'world wide web' or the internet. The internet was first made available to universities in 1989 but by the mid-90s almost the entire country had a range of Internet Service Providers (ISPs). Nobody in their wildest dreams could have envisioned back then what the result on society might be.

The Commodore 64. Most of us started our computer journey with one of these.

Wikipedia

And what about your first computer? When did you venture into the digital world?

Your first journey into the digital world of computers was probably on something like a Commodore 64.

Although these days it looks like an unimpressive keyboard-like box, the Commodore C64 was incredibly popular. It was first released in 1982 and more C64s have been sold than any other single computer system, even to this day. *The Guinness Book of World Records* calls it the best selling comuter model of all time.

It seems amazing when you look around today at the impressive array of desktop computers, laptops, tablets and smart phones when just over 30 years ago, very few people had anything to do with computers.

What are some of your memories of your first encounter with a computer?

Chopping the wood for the wood stove was usually the boy's job. Protective eyewear hadn't been thought of back then either.

iStock

Lighting the fire last night, I was thinking back to the days when we would have a load of wood delivered several times during the year, and my job, as a kid, was to cut the kindling.

We needed wood for the stove and the copper and there was a fireplace in the sitting room. There was a woodheap at the bottom of the yard and when the wood was delivered it had to be stacked and covered with a big canvas tarp. Every couple of days Dad would cut up the wood needed and stack it neatly next to the wood stove ready for use.

I doubt parents would let an 8- or 9-year-old kid use a sharp axe these days (and without protective glasses), not to mention flying chips of wood and splinters, but back then it was seen as teaching kids to be responsible and it was my job to keep up the kindling.

Woodheaps were pretty scary too with lots of spiders and the odd snake or lizard.

Remember when you had to cut the wood?

When I was a kid I built a crystal radio set. I think I got the idea from a *Boy's Own Annual* and sent away for all the bits. I strapped a piece of wire across the roof and clipped an alligator clip to the water pipe. I used to listen to the wireless for hours.

You could build the whole thing yourself and although you had to listen with headphones it was so exciting!

I was trying to explain to someone much younger how a crystal set works and he couldn't quite grasp the fact you didn't need any electricity or battery.

Anybody else have a crystal set?

My first radio was a crystal set, which I built with my Dad's help, from instructions in *Boy's Own*.

Wikimedia Commons

The ice man came with a big block of ice for the ice chest every second or third day in summer.

Courtesy of Cheryl Dianne McPhee

Cheryl Dianne McPhee sent this photo to share: 'Who remembers ice being delivered? My Dad owned an ice round, and this is me on his truck.'

Back in the '50s, before refrigerators, we had ice chests where all the perishables were stored and every couple of days the ice man would call with a big block of ice for the top of the chest.

He would carry it inside with a pair of ice tongs and put it in the ice chest.

If it was hot he used to give all the kids a chip of ice each. I remember too, as the boy in our family, it was my job to carry out the tray that sat under the ice chest to catch the water from the melted ice.

Remember your ice man?

Harry's Cafe de Wheels in Woolloomooloo is an institution in Sydney and over the years has become quite a tourist attraction.

It was set up by Harry 'Tiger' Edwards as a pie cart near the northern wharf end of Cowper Wharf Road, Potts Point, to provide hot snacks for the Navy sailors. Harry wasn't there for long before he joined the Army and was injured during World War II.

When he came back he reopened his little caravan and it soon became a tradition, a 'must visit' for the sailors, and Harry did very well indeed.

In 1974, chicken king Colonel Sanders stopped at Harry's and enjoyed the food so much that he ate three 'pies and peas' while leaning on his walking stick in front of the caravan.

Elton John has also been a visitor to Harry's over the years and held a press conference from inside Harry's during the 1970s.

Harry operated the caravan for a further 30 years before selling the business to Alex Kuronya in 1975.

Harry's first pie cart (pictured here) is now at the Powerhouse Museum in Sydney.

Harry's Cafe de Wheels was an institution in Sydney.

Powerhouse Museum Sydney

Albert Namatjira of the Western Arrente people at Hermannsburg became a household name during the 1950s as Australia's most successful Aboriginal artist. His watercolours were a complete departure from the abstract designs and symbols of traditional Aboriginal art.

By the mid-1960s, prints of Namatjira's paintings hung in thousands of Australian homes. His watercolours usually highlighted the landscape of the MacDonnell Ranges and its distinctive flora with very old, stately and majestic white gum trees surrounded by twisted scrub.

Using colours similar to the ochres of his ancestors, his style was very much Western. Soon after he passed away, some critics panned his unique style as they thought it reflected his assimilation into Western culture. However, Namatjira is now considered one of Australia's greatest artists as well as a pioneer of Aboriginal rights.

Because of his enormous success he was the first Northern Territory Aboriginal person to be freed from restrictions that made Aboriginal people wards of the state. In 1957, he became the first Indigenous person to be granted restricted Australian citizenship, which allowed him to vote, have limited land rights and buy alcohol. In 1956 his portrait, by William Dargie, won the Archibald Prize. Namatjira was also awarded the Queen's Coronation Medal in 1953.

He died from heart disease in 1959 – and although poor at the time of his death, he left a legacy of around 2000 artworks.

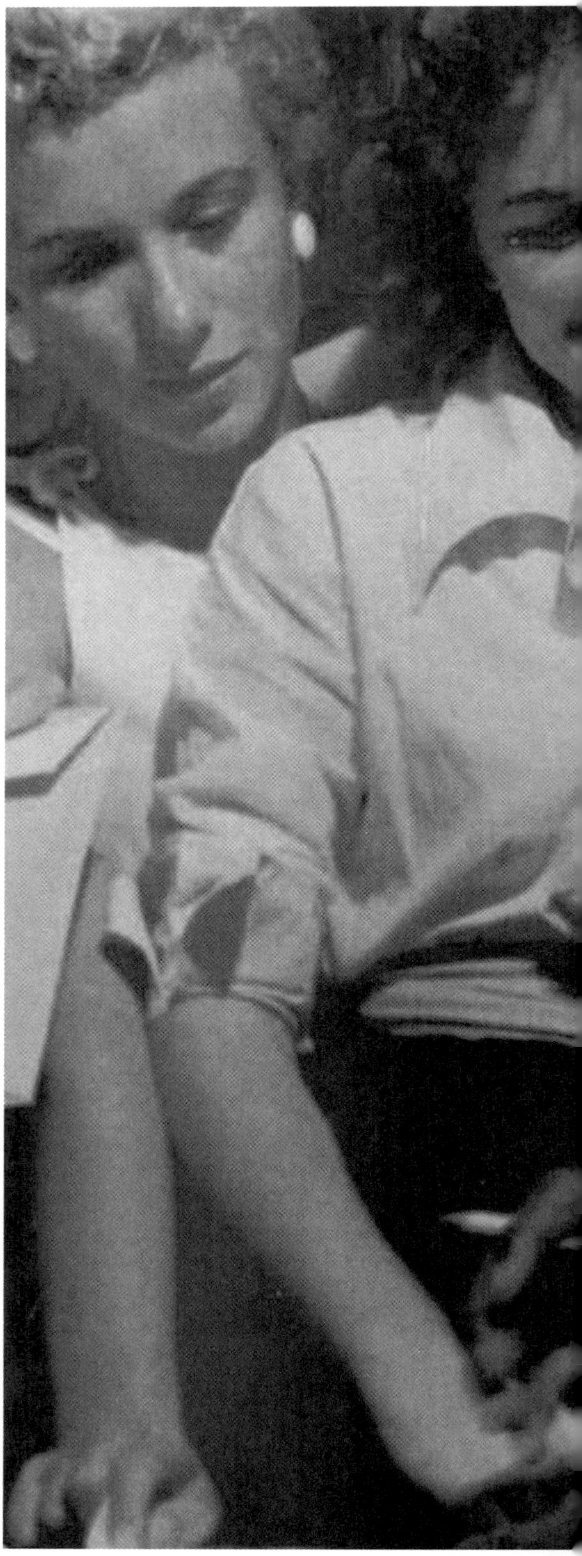

Indigenous Australian artist Albert Namatjira, signing autographs.

National Library of Australia, PIC/7569/51

Junket was not my favourite desert. I loved my Mum's bread and butter puddings with custard, though.

Courtesy of Kerrin Light

It had been a while since I'd thought of junket when Kerrin Light sent this photo to me. 'I remember this stuff as a child. My grandmother made it for us. It was awful. I found these in the back of my mother-in-law's pantry cupboard many years ago. Who else remembers having junket?'

Uggh ... Yes, junket was pretty awful I recall. There was worse, though! Remember blancmange, which was a bit like junket with less taste? I also hated sago pudding but loved bread and butter pudding. And I guess the favourite was homemade ice cream.

What are some of the desserts you can remember mum or grandma making?

The popular sandwich spread Vegemite would come in small glass jars, which once emptied were recycled as children's drinking glasses.

As kids, we never drank out of the 'good' glasses (which were saved for special occasions), but had a set of mis-matched smaller drinking glasses that had originally been the glass jar for the Vegemite. It was a very clever marketing approach by Kraft-Walker, the makers of Vegemite.

Interesting to look back now at how frugal our parents were. As my Grandma used to say ... 'waste not, want not'!

From the early 1950s Vegemite was sold in re-usable drinking glasses. We were all 'Happy Little Vegemites'.

Museum of Applied Arts & Sciences

#18 FACT

There is one food that is only eaten by Australians – Vegemite! We buy 22 million jars of it each year. Did you know that in 2017 ownership of Vegemite returned to Australian hands when dairy company Bega bought it from the US company that owns Kraft?

An after-school snack of Vita Weat biscuits and Vegemite worms.

YouTube

Suzi Catchpole from 'The Essential Kid' blog laments the fact that it's now impossible to make 'Vita Weat' worms from the childhood staple biscuits, Arnott's Vita-Weats.

> There probably wasn't a single kid of the '80s with a TV, who didn't know that catchy jingle off by heart. At the 17 second mark there's the iconic image of the young boy squeezing his Vegemite and butter worms through those fabled Vita-Weat holes. Perfect curly worms rearing their heads, then curling as they grew longer and finally destroyed with a lick of the tongue.
>
> There's a ritual involved when eating Vita-Weats; it's as much a part of me as Vegemite, as the smell of (the now maligned) Reef Oil in summer, of the rush of wind through my hair as I ride a bike.

I can only agree Suzi.

An Ansett Boeing 727-100 at Sydney Airport in 1970.

Wikipedia, photo John Wheatley

Icons of our era – Ansett Airlines. It was on 5 March 2002 that Ansett Airlines made its final flight, AN152, from Perth to Sydney.

Founded by Sir Reginald Myles 'Reg' Ansett in 1935, Ansett had been a significant player in the Australian domestic airline scene for nearly seven decades.

Back on 17 February 1936, the very first flight – a single engine Fokker Universal – departed Hamilton, Victoria, bound for Melbourne.

In the 1990s, Air New Zealand became a 50 per cent shareholder of Ansett and eventually went on to acquire full ownership in February 2000. Unfortunately, due to some poor business decisions, Ansett became more of a liability than an asset and in September 2001 Air New Zealand placed the Ansett group of companies into voluntary administration. Sadly 16 000 people lost their jobs.

During the 1960s and '70s, Australia followed the United States and much of Europe and embraced the Women's Liberation Movement.

As the television industry expanded throughout the post-war years, and access to higher education for both women and men improved, an awareness of the social problems women faced and the need for a cultural change came to the fore as never before. As women became more educated and joined the work force, many jobs which had been traditionally 'men only' were taken on by women.

Unfortunately, this new awareness didn't dent the inequality around the number of hours women spent on domestic responsibilities. Despite the fact that families increasingly depended on two incomes, women carried most of the domestic work and care of children.

In 1972, Helen Reddy's song, 'I Am Woman' captured the mood of this social change more than any other.

It was a changing world back in 1975 when Melbourne got its first ever lady tram drivers, Joyce Barry and Cath Stone.

Photo by News Ltd/Newspix

It's known as the 'Flying Kangaroo' and as 'Australia's Own Airline' and is one of the oldest airlines in the world.

Qantas stands for Queensland and Northern Territory Aerial Services and was founded in Winton, Queensland in 1920. Initially it was a small airline operating taxi and joy flights but in 1934 Qantas Empire Airways Limited (QEA) was formed by Qantas and Britain's Imperial Airways. They flew internationally from May 1935, when the service from Darwin was extended to Singapore.

In 1947, QEA was nationalised, with the Australian government buying the shares, and in the same year the airline took delivery of its first Lockheed L-749 Constellation and took over the trunk route to London.

In 1958, Qantas became the second round-the-world airline, flying Super Constellations from Australia to London through Asia and the Middle East. It still retains its reputation as one of the safest airlines in the world.

Qantas Boeing 707 arriving at Heathrow from Australia in 1959.

Alamy

QANTAS
VH-EBD
AUSTRALIA'S OVERSEAS AIRLI
707

The last man to be hanged in Australia was in 1967. Ronald Ryan flanked by two detectives after his recapture in January 1966.

Photo by News Ltd/Newspix

At the height of the Cold War, Australians awoke one morning in April 1954 to find themselves at the centre of a diplomatic storm with the Soviet Republic.

That morning photos in the newspapers showed Mrs Evdokia Petrov being forced onto a waiting plane by two very thuggish-looking men attempting to kidnap her and return her to Russia.

The Petrovs had been working in Canberra as diplomats, but were in fact undercover Soviet spies. After Stalin's death Vladimir Petrov feared he would be sent to Siberia so he contacted ASIO offering to tell all in exchange for political asylum. The Russians immediately sent a couple of henchmen to Australia to kidnap his wife Evdokia.

The dramatic photos of Mrs Petrov being manhandled by KGB agents at the airport that day have become iconic images of 1950s Australia in the Cold War. When the plane landed in Darwin for refuelling, Federal Police freed Mrs Petrov.

Evdokia Petrova at Mascot Airport, Sydney, loses her shoe as she is 'escorted' across the tarmac to a waiting plane by two armed Russian diplomatic couriers.

Photo by News Ltd/Newspix

Ronald Ryan was the last person to be legally executed in Australia at 8 am on Friday, 3 February 1967. He had been found guilty of shooting and killing prison warder George Hodson during an escape from Pentridge Prison two years earlier in 1965.

There was much discussion at the time as to whether Ryan was even guilty of the crime as there was a strong case to suggest that Officer Hodson had died as the result of an accidental shot from another warder's gun.

The Premier of Victoria at the time, Henry Bolte, was not swayed by some of the largest public protests in the history of Australia and allowed the hanging to proceed in the end.

The death penalty was abolished in all states of Australia by 1985.

Very few Australians have had a bigger impact on Australian history than Sir Keith Murdoch. Today many people will immediately identify him as the father of Rupert Murdoch, founder and chairman of News Corp, one of the biggest media companies in the world.

But Keith Murdoch is a much more important figure in our story.

Sir Keith's career in journalism covered almost the entire first half of the twentieth century. He decided at a young age that he should aim to be 'useful in the world'. It was an ambition that he pursued with a rare single-mindedness.

He rose from a frugal background and overcame shyness and a speech impediment to become affluent in a competitive society. He was a journalist of rare distinction, writer of the famed Gallipoli Letter that alerted governments to the disasters unfolding on the Turkish battlefields and in peacetime a leader within the newspaper industry.

Sir Keith Murdoch died at his property, Cruden Farm, in October 1952. His wife, Dame Elizabeth, died in 2012.

Keith Arthur Murdoch.

National Library of Australia, nla.obj-231555508-e

#19 FACT

Australia has the world's longest fence. It's also one of the longest structures on the planet! Extending from Jimbour, Queensland, to the Eyre Peninsula in South Australia, the Dingo Fence runs a staggering 5614 kilometres across three states. It has helped reduce losses of sheep to predators. Australia is also home to the world's second longest fence – Western Australia's rabbit-proof fence.

How many times did you get your fingers caught when setting one of these old mousetraps?

There is a great story behind this Aussie creation. Arnold Standfield from Kyogle in northern New South Wales searched junkyards during World War II to find scrap metal to build a trap-making machine. The 'machine' came about in 1943 and was used up to the '90s. The original traps he created were often repaired but never replaced. There is an original mousetrap on display at the Powerhouse Museum in Sydney.

An original old mousetrap.

Courtesy of Peter's Milk Bar

Bill Williams (now 90 years old) sent a photo: 'In my last year at the Clarendon School, in 1940, I used to sell dressed rabbits for 6d to three loyal customers in Clarendon, delivering them on the way to school. In 1941, having left school, I used traps to catch rabbits, but mainly used a ferret to hunt them from their warrens into nets, also shooting some, selling their skins.'

Thanks Bill. We were a more rural society back then and kids I believe had a much clearer understanding of animals and their role in our lives.

Rabbits were a nuisance and we learned how to set traps or took out the .22 and went spotlighting. After we killed the rabbits we would then skin them and sell the pelts while Mum would cook up a rabbit stew for tea.

I often look at kids today and wonder how they would survive if they were suddenly transported back to the '40s or '50s ... Come to think of it I probably wouldn't survive myself!

Bill Williams shown here at age 13, in 1941, with his dog, ferret, gun and rabbits he caught near Clarendon. He would sell their skins.

Courtesy of Bill Williams

Just looking at the photo I can almost smell the perfume again.

eBay

Lesley Bligh sent this photo with the comment: 'I remember this face cream smell like it was yesterday. My grandmother always used this lotion on her face and hands. Oil of Olay doesn't measure up in the scent department.'

Thanks, Lesley. There's a bit of discussion about this product on the internet. It's now called Oil of Olay in Australia but in some other countries it's still Ulan. It's Oil of Olay in America too, Oil of Ulay in the UK and some of Europe, Oil of Ulag in other parts, and finally, Oil of Ulaz in the rest!

Maybe copyright issues, but I certainly remember the days when it was Oil of Ulan, and I can definitely remember that smell!

Seeing this Cashmere Bouquet Gift Pack reminds me of the gifts we used to buy Mum at Christmas or on her birthday.

We never got much pocket money, and whatever we did get went on lollies or Saturday afternoon at the flicks, so saving up to buy Mum or Dad a present was always difficult.

However, we'd somehow scrape up enough and go into town to purchase the present and after very careful consideration and umming and ahhing, we'd settle on something that looked nice, smelt nice and wasn't too expensive ... The ideal gift for a much-loved Mum.

Memories of buying my Mum a Mother's Day gift.

eBay

The mid-'60s brought about a more playful approach to hair and make-up and the use of colour, voluminous hair, lots of eyeliner and mini-skirts.

Some of our readers even remember ironing their hair and as one recalled, 'I loved being young in the '60s, being 17 at the Beatles' concert at the Sydney Stadium, having a hairstyle as in this photo, wearing mini-skirts with lots of eyeliner, going overseas and visiting the Kings Road and Carnaby Street with such great gear!'

The beehive, a modern hairstyle circa 1960s. Stefanie Powers from 'The New Interns'.

Alamy

#20 FACT

The 1977 Grand Final had one of the most dramatic endings in AFL history. The Kangaroos, coached by the legendary Ron Barassi, were up against Collingwood. When the final siren sounded the scores were level at 76 points each. North Melbourne won the re-match the following week. In a great coincidence, Parramatta and St George also tied in their 1977 Rugby League Grand Final. The Dragons won that replay 22-0. Unforgettable!

Rod Laver is widely regarded by many to be the greatest tennis player Australia has ever produced and one of the greatest players in the history of the sport.

He was ranked No. 1 from 1964 to 1970 and his 200 singles titles are the most won by a single player in tennis history. This includes his all-time men's record of 10 or more titles per year for seven consecutive years (1964–70). He excelled on all of the court surfaces of the time: grass, clay, hard, carpet and wood/parquet.

Rod won 11 Grand Slam singles titles, and is the only player to twice achieve the calendar-year Grand Slam, in 1962 and 1969. He also won eight Pro Slam titles, including the 'pro Grand Slam' in 1967, and he contributed to five Davis Cup titles for Australia during an age when the Davis Cup was deemed as significant as the Grand Slams.

Australian tennis player Rod Laver at the 1969 Top Tennis Tournament in Amsterdam.

Evers, Joost/Anefo, National Archives of the Netherlands

SPECIAL
GERALDINE

Ron Blaskett was a famous ventriloquist back in the '50s and'60s, and with his doll Gerry Gee, became a household name. He was a regular on radio and TV programs such as *The Tarax Show*, *IMT* and *Young Talent Time*.

Ron travelled the world, playing at the 1975 Toronto Expo, for Cyclone Tracy victims in Darwin and Diggers in Vietnam.

Although he retired in 1999 he was easily talked into a comeback by fond fans in 2000, and has ridden the nostalgia wave since then, working clubs and nursing homes.

Last I heard of Ron is that he really, really retired in 2012.

Remember Ron and Gerry on TV all those years ago?

Ron Blaskett and his ventriloquist dolls.

Museums Victoria. Reg. No: MM 131953

School holidays at the beach, sandcastles and a bush biscuit.

Pinterest

What about those fantastic school holidays at the beach?

Building castles in the sand, mucking around in the water, having a Bush biscuit for lunch with lashings of butter and Vegemite, washed down with a bottle of Coke from the little beach kiosk.

We used to ride our bikes to the beach on a hot sunny day, no hat, no sunscreen, no crash helmet and stop at every public telephone box along the way to press Button B, just in case we got lucky.

All day at the beach, red as a lobster we'd ride home (had to be there before the street lights came on), and Mum would slice up a tomato and put it on my back to stop the blisters. Can't remember, but I don't think it worked very well!

The local greengrocer drove a truck with fresh fruit and vegetables for sale.

Home delivery via handy apps is one of the fastest-growing industries in Australia today, but delivery to the door is not really new; it's just making a comeback.

Instead of being revolutionised by the internet, home delivery after World War I was transformed by motorised transport.

Today, the deliveries – parcels, pre-packed meals and groceries – arrive sporadically via faceless couriers.

But in the late 1950s, you could just about set your watch by the delivery men (yes, all were male). Daily pre-dawn regulars were the milko and paper man, mid-morning the postie, noon the baker and late-arvo the paperboy. The greengrocer usually came once a week and all the mums in the neighbourhood would gather around the truck and buy their weekly supplies.

Fruit and vegetables would be carefully selected, mostly locally grown and in season. Before the miracle of refrigeration and cold storage, most of the produce probably came from local growers.

The selected items would then be placed in paper bags or wrapped in yesterday's newspaper and paid for in cash.

Some of these mobile greengrocers had a regular fruit and vegetable barrow situated in high traffic areas around the city. As a child I recall a fruit/veg barrow outside the local railway station which was there for many years.

The rise of the supermarket saw the demise of these little businesses.

Fred Ellers' Chrysler truck full of fruit and veges from Dalkeith, Western Australia in 1929.

State Library of Western Australia, 100354PD

FELLERS
DALKEITH STORE

Dr James Wright, also known as 'The Merry Medic'.

Courtesy of Celebrity Speakers

Dr James Wright, 'The Merry Medic', was a popular segment on the radio and TV in the '70s and '80s.

His real name is Dr John Franklin Knight but back in the day when he started out on radio he wasn't allowed to go by his real name so he became Dr James Wright.

He started out writing for a women's magazine in 1968 and over the years has written many books, newspaper columns and articles for numerous publications as well as appearing on TV. He's been on so many different television shows over the years, he became known as the Media Medic. He's also called 'The Merry Medic' because he gave medical advice and health tips in simple everyday language anybody can understand with the ever-present smile on his face.

He's now over 90, but age hasn't slowed him down at all. He published a memoir in 2016 and continues to write health advice columns and can still be heard on the radio.

#21 FACT

Australia's Medicare was first introduced in 1975 by the Whitlam government as Medibank. In 1976, it was limited to paying customers only by the Fraser government but Bob Hawke reintroduced universal health care in 1984. We've all had a Medicare card in our wallets ever since.

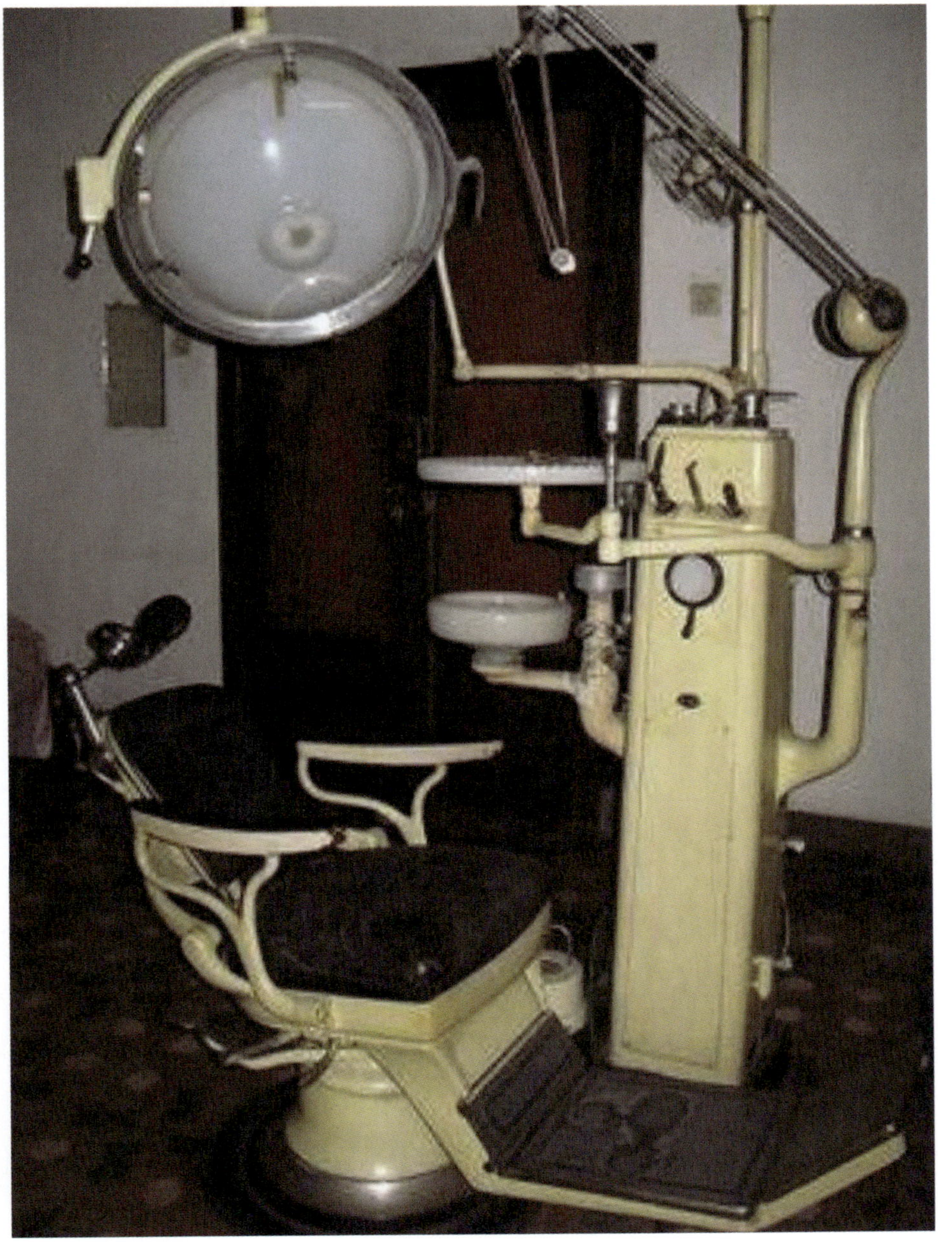

It looks more like a torture chamber today but this is what faced us at the dentist in the 'good old days'.

Courtesy of Ian Keith Kershaw

Ian Keith Kershaw shared a photo and some not so pleasant memories of the good old days: 'Anyone remember the slow torture chamber of the 1950s?'

Sends chills down my spine when I recall my first trip to the dentist as a kid back in the '50s. In fact I still hate going to the dentist today.

Dentistry has come a long way since the bad old days (thankfully). What are your memories of going to the dentist as a child?

'Tan Don't Burn, Use Coppertone' – the famous Coppertone ad.

Courtesy of Bayer

The old Coppertone ad would be seen as very inappropriate these days, but ran for years around Australia, selling the tanning lotion.

Every summer, almost every kid, at some stage, would end up with a severe case of sunburn ... no blockout with SPF 30 or 50 back then! Mum would administer slices of cold tomato (cold tea was another favourite) but basically it was a matter of suffering in silence and waiting for the blisters to break or go down.

Thank goodness we know so much more about skin care these days. I can't ever remember wearing a hat when I was a kid – how about you?

This was another favourite outdoor game from school: leapfrog.

Hopscotch, pick-up sticks, skipping – the list of the old schoolyard favourites could go on forever but how many of these once loved games do kids still play today?

What about hide-and-seek, knucklebones (jacks), marbles, Simon says, blind man's bluff, what's the time, Mr Wolf?, red rover, etc? And not forgetting kicking the footy around, basketball and backyard or street cricket.

What were some of your favourite schoolyard or neighbourhood games growing up?

Leapfrog was another of those very energetic games we all played.

Pinterest

Having a good 'mix tape' of all your favourite songs was very satisfying!

iStock

Making a good mix tape was an art. You had to sit at your boombox, finger poised and triggered to press record at the exact moment the radio DJ stops talking and the song begins, hoping the DJ shuts up in time to catch the intro.

Oh yes ... in these days of pre-release single downloads on iTunes, streaming previews and leaked copies of albums doing the rounds in advance, it seems rather quaint to think that you had to rely on the radio for new music.

Can you recall as a budding music fan, when a favourite artist had a new single coming out, the only way to get a copy in advance was to record it from the radio?

In the late '50s, 45s and 33s had just come in, replacing the 78rpm records.

My very first single was 'Hound Dog' by Elvis Presley and from then on I was forever hooked on music.

My first LP was *Paul Anka*, by Paul Anka of course, which I still have and can now play again having just bought a new digitally enhanced record player (yep, vinyl records are making a big comeback).

What do you remember about your local record shop? And what was your first 45 and LP record?

A record shop with all the latest music on sale.

Wikipedia, photo Jahidalgoaloy

1970s

KENTON
jazz
GENE AMMONS TENOR SAX FAVORITES
BENNY CARTER
LATIN
ROCK
JAZZ
SOUL
AGUSTIN
LARA
Hello, Dolly!
uis Armstrong

Who remembers using the old Gestetner machines at school?

As I recall, the Gestetner was around long before photocopiers. A thin sheet of paper coated with wax was written on with a special stylus, which would leave a broken line through the stencil. This broke the paper, removing the wax covering, forcing ink through the stencil – originally by an ink roller – which would then leave its impression.

Some of the copying machines had a very strong ink/alcohol smell and I think we used to get a bit high on the fumes. All gone now, of course, replaced by computers and photocopiers.

Before photocopiers and copy machines we had the Gestetner.

Wikipedia, photo Goldfinger

Ian Keith Kershaw shared some memories and a photo: 'Telegrams were once sent over a distance by Morse code before teleprinters. This model of telegraph was probably the first type of digital transmission.

The message everyone knows is SOS: dit dit dit dah dah dah dit dit dit on a Morse Key like this one of brass and bakelite made by Clipsal.'

When I first started working at the PMG Department in the late 1950s, Morse code was still regularly used if the teleprinter network failed.

Morse code was first invented in 1836 and was still taught to Boy Scouts and Girl Guides as late as the early 1960s but with the arrival of the digital age it is no longer used.

I can still recall the pain of trying to learn the Morse code at Boy Scouts or Girl Guides.

Courtesy of Ian Keith Kershaw

#22 FACT

Even with mass post-war migration from Europe, the White Australia Policy shaped the way our country looked in the 1950s and 1960s. It would be dismantled over the next decades: the *Migration Act* of 1956 abolished the controversial dictation test and in 1966 Harold Holt's government opened up migration to non-Europeans. Since the 1970s our migration policy has been non-discriminatory on the basis of race, ethnicity or religion.

How do you remember Joh Bjelke-Petersen?

Joh was the longest-serving Premier of Queensland, holding office from 1968 to 1987, during which time the state enjoyed considerable economic development, though many called Queensland a police state.

His uncompromising conservatism, crackdowns on dissent, political longevity, and his leadership of a government that was revealed to be institutionally corrupt through the Fitzgerald Inquiry, made him one of the best-known and most controversial political figures of 20th-century Australia.

Despite consistently receiving the smallest number of votes out of Queensland's leading three parties, Bjelke-Petersen's Country (later National) Party controlled the state. This peculiar result was achieved through a notorious system of electoral gerrymander that resulted in rural votes having greater value than those from city electorates.

Although nicknamed the 'Hillbilly Dictator', he was hughely popular with conservative voters and over the course of his 19 years as premier he tripled the number of people who voted for his party and doubled the party's percentage vote.

In 1985, he unsuccessfully launched a campaign to move into federal politics with the aim of becoming Prime Minister. Born in New Zealand, he died in Kingaroy, Queensland in 2005 at the age of 94.

Hate him or love him, Joh was a political force always to be reckoned with. I wonder how he would fare in politics today.

Joh Bjelke-Petersen was a political force in Australia as the Premier of Queensland.

Courtesy of the Liberal National Party, Queensland

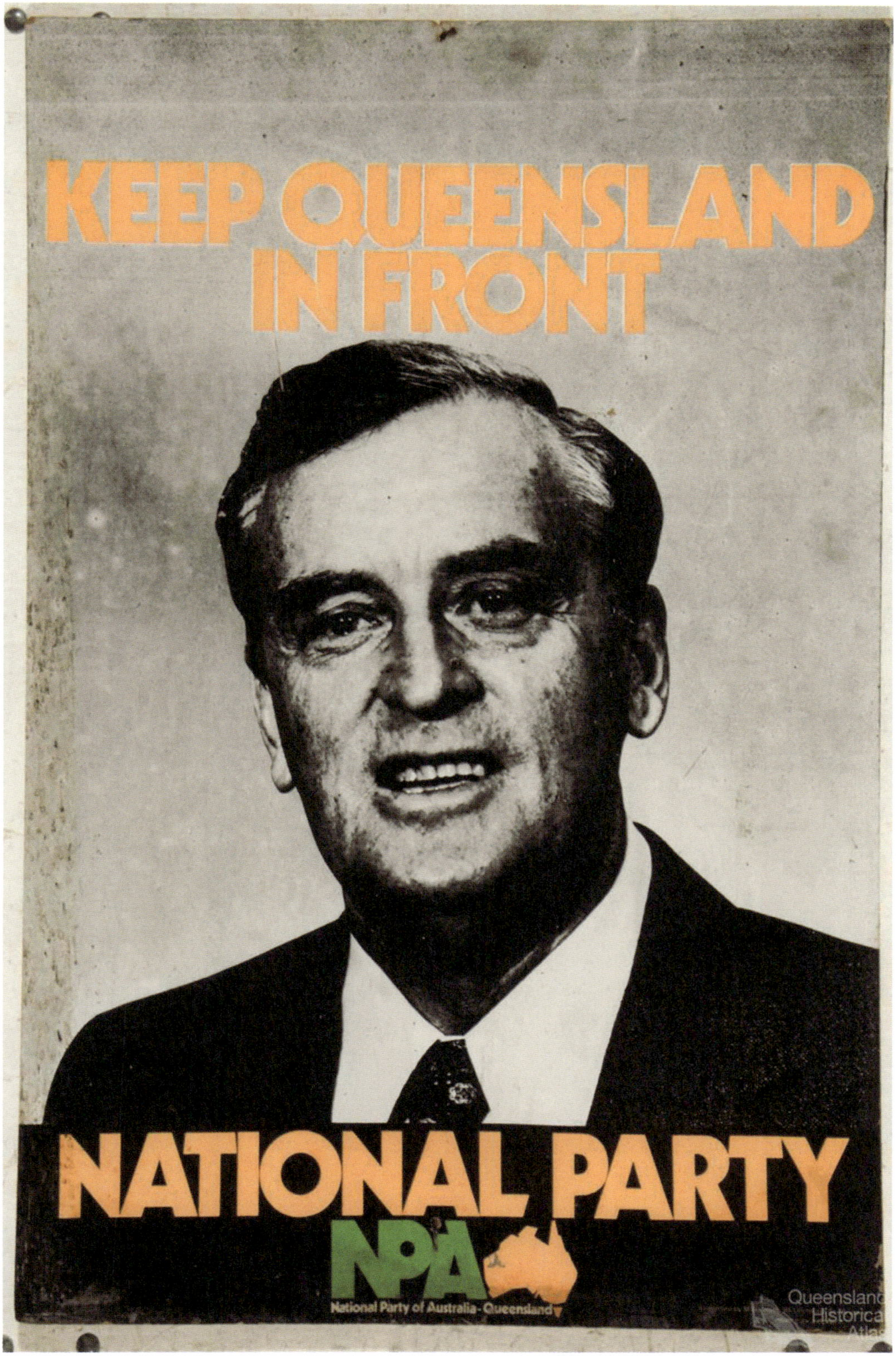
KEEP QUEENSLAND
IN FRONT
NATIONAL PARTY
NPA
National Party of Australia - Queensland
Queensland
Historical
Atlas

The hand-operated clippers would come out when it was time for the kids to get a haircut.

Courtesy of Ray Wellington

Ray Wellington shared a photo: 'Remember when it was that dreaded time when Mum or Dad would announce "It's about time all you kids had a haircut. Who's first?"'

Ahhh, that brings back memories. We had a set of these clippers. Although I can still recall as a kid going to the local barber for a haircut. His name was Mr Sullivan and he had a really narrow little shop with the barber's chair down the back and a row of seats on both sides. Behind the chair was a counter from where he sold cigarettes and tobacco.

I can still remember the hair oil smell in the shop. Do you remember getting a 'short back and sides' when you were a kid?

1950s Scotch Tape ad.

Imgur

1954

TRIMS
FRINGES
Fix fringe to forehead with "SCOTCH" Tape and cut across top of tape. Fringe cuts straight, hair trimmings stick to tape — won't fall in eyes. "SCOTCH" Brand Cellulose Tape is your handiest household helper.
ALWAYS ASK FOR
TRADE MARK
SCOTCH
BRAND
CELLULOSE
TAPE

PLAY
SCHOOL
Noni
Hazlehurst
ABC TV

Australia's first-ever female Gold Logie winner was Lorrae Desmond, probably best remembered for the role as Shirley Gilroy in *A Country Practice*. Lorrae won the coveted award in 1962 for the *Lorrae Desmond Show*. Now 83, Lorrae recalled recently:

> In those early Logies, Graham Kennedy seemed to win the Gold every year. I've always made lists of the things I want to achieve and I put winning the Gold on that list. I was working on TV in both Australia and England at the time and *The Lorrae Desmond Show* was doing well on the ABC. I then headed to the US for a while and it was while I was in Hollywood that I won the Gold Logie. I was thrilled when I ticked that achievement off my list – and was the first woman to do so, as well!

She won a Logie for playing Shirley Gilroy too. Do you remember Shirley from *A Country Practice*?

A Country Practice, everybody's favourite Australian TV show, ran for 12 years. Lorrae Desmond played the role of Shirley Gilroy.

ATN 7

Amy Koenen-Phillips was having a bit of a clean-up recently and discovered this publicity shot from the ABC and *Play School* and decided to share it. Memories of Noni Hazelhurst, who was a *Play School* presenter from 1978 to 2002, and has been a National Ambassador or Patron for many children's charities.

'An '80s flashback from Play School.'

Courtesy of the ABC

Noni Hazlehurst is an actress, director, writer, presenter and broadcaster who has appeared on television and radio, in dramas, mini-series and made for television films, as well as on stage and in feature films since the early 1970s.

Noni has been honoured with numerous awards including Australian Film Institute awards, ARIA awards and Logies, including being inducted into the Hall of Fame in 2016.

These were the good old days of fun TV with programs like *Hey Hey It's Saturday* and its popular segment Red Faces.

Red Faces actually turned up some pretty good acts occasionally although they were mostly just funny or bloody awful. It was always good for a laugh though and I remember sometimes the judging panel would include an international guest as a judge who had no idea that the entire segment was a send-up and would be embarrassed by the whole experience. Aussie humour at its finest!

Red Symons always played such a meanie but it was good fun, light entertainment TV that we don't get all that much on the telly anymore.

Red Faces was my favourite segment on TV's *Hey Hey It's Saturday*.

Courtesy of Hey Hey It's Saturday

RED FACES

Graham Kennedy in the 1970s hosting an episode of *Blankety Blanks*.

Courtesy of Fremantle Media

Talking about the early days of TV in Australia, who remembers *Matlock Police*?

Made by Crawford Productions for the 0-10 Network (now known as the Ten Network) between 1971 and 1976, *Matlock Police* was an Australian TV police drama series. Based in the Victorian town of Matlock and the surrounding district, the series focused on crime in the area as well as the police station and its policemen.

On 22 February 1971 the first epispde was screened in black and white, until the series switched to colour in the 'Loggerheads' episode – the 162nd episode.

Matlock Police was cancelled in 1975 after 229 episodes.

Matlock Police focused on the police station and crime in the Victorian town of Matlock and the surrounding district.

Courtesy of Crawford Productions

Trent Mckinnon sent a photo: '"*Blankety Blanks* is an Australian game show based on the American game show *Match Game*. It was hosted by Graham Kennedy on Network Ten from 1977–1978. Wikipedia".'

Thanks, Trent. What an incredible TV performer Graham Kennedy was. Certainly the best we've ever seen in Australia and one of the greatest of all time.

Blankety Blanks was a perfect platform for his comedy and although it only ran for two seasons, '77 and '78, it was extremely popular and very funny!

Its awards included the Gold Logie for Best Personality on Australian Television for Graham Kennedy and the Logie for Most Popular Variety Program.

The *Mother and Son* TV series starred Garry McDonald and Ruth Cracknell.

Courtesy of the ABC

Another in the series of favourite Australian TV programs.

I'm sure you'll remember *Mother and Son*, the sitcom produced by the ABC from 1984 until 1994. The show starred Ruth Cracknell, Garry McDonald, Henri Szeps and Judy Morris, plus many Australian actors of the time in guest roles.

The plot centred around the problems of ageing and caring for somebody with increasing memory loss, with clever humour and a tinge of sadness. Despite the subject matter, the show was an audience favourite right around the country.

Garry McDonald's portrayal of Arthur was outstanding while the performance of Ruth Cracknell as Maggie was particularly lauded as one of the finest characterisations on Australian television. The series itself became extremely popular and has screened in constant reruns, particularly by Network Ten.

#23

FACT

In 1954, Bob Hawke set a world record for sculling a yard of ale (2.5 pints of beer) in 11 seconds. Hawke's record was immortalised by the Guinness Book of Records. Affectionately nicknamed 'The Silver Bodgie', Bob later suggested that this was the reason for his great political success as it endeared him to his electorate. He was Prime Minister from 1983 to 1991, the longest serving Labor prime minister.

Another great Australian invention – the Victa motorised lawn mower.

Wikimedia Commons, photo fir0002

The latest model motor mower runs on batteries! It's a far cry from the early '50s when the great Aussie invention the Victa lawn mower made its debut.

It was invented in 1952, in the backyard of Mervyn Victor Richardson in Concord, NSW.

Mervyn's son, Garry, mowed lawns to earn money in university holidays and Mervyn wanted to design a new mower for his son's business. In August 1952 he decided to make a rotary lawn mower out of scrap metal. By 1953, demand was so strong that Richardson gave up his job and became full-time manager of Victa Mowers Pty Ltd.

Since 1952, Victa has sold over eight million lawn mowers in 30 countries. In later years, the company was bought by American-based Briggs & Stratton.

David Fausset posted a memory: 'Who remembers Joe from Nock and Kirby's in the '70s/early '80s? Channel 9 Saturdays? "Bring your money with you. Bye bye now."'

Joe the Gadget Man (real name, Joe Sandow) used to appear on Australian TV every Saturday morning after 11 am for Nock and Kirby's: 'And ladies, not only does it dice, it makes lovely shoestring chips!'

Joe showed you the basics for making a decent feed, painting the door on your garage and maybe putting up some shelving and that was it. Australians were quite taken with the advent of black-and-white television in 1956 and Joe's demonstrations and patter soon had a loyal following.

'Bring your money with you,' became his catchcry. Joe passed away on Saturday 26 October 2002. He was 89.

Joe the Gadget Man from Nock and Kirby's.

YouTube

Courtesy Bauer Media Pty Limited / The Australian Women's Weekly

Our trikes and bikes were generally handed on from one sibling to the other. Very few kids had new bikes or trikes.

eBay

My first trike would have been handed down from my elder sister. Are toys still handed down from sibling to sibling as they were back when we were kids?

I recall my father gave it a fresh coat of paint and blackened the pedals and tyres with black shoe polish. Most of the big gifts or presents we got as kids were secondhand. As a single-income family back in those days, parents did not have a lot of money to spend on expensive gifts. When it came time for us to get the two wheeler it was secondhand as well.

I wonder how many kids get secondhand bikes these days?

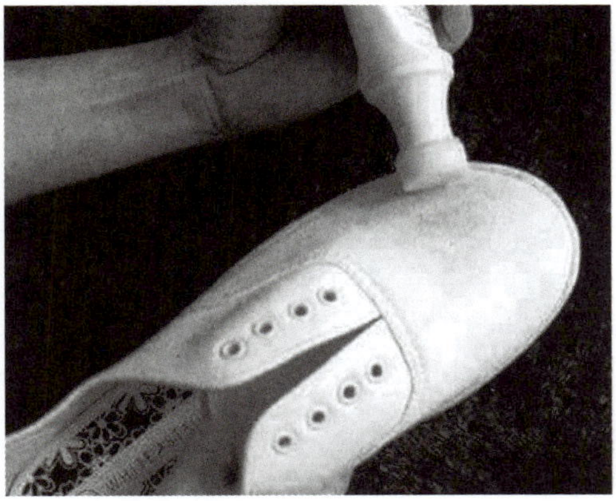

One of our Friday night jobs was to whiten the sandshoes for Saturday sport.

Pinterest

A very important part of the weekly routine was whitening your sand shoes. Long before the days of upmarket runners like Nike and Adidas, we wore all-white sand shoes like Dunlop Volleys (remember those?), and once a week, before PE day, or playing tennis on the weekend, we had to whiten them with Kiwi Shoe Whitener.

I still remember the distinctive smell of the stuff! And we always had to lay out two sheets of newspaper to make sure we didn't stain the good lino ... We'd wear the same sand shoes for anything to do with sports, running, tennis, cricket and school PE. I can't recall any padding to absorb shock in those shoes either, we were tough kids back then!

Ahhh, memories.

Kim Bell posted a photo and shared some of the history of this famous shoe:

> On sports day at school we would all wear the same shoes – our Dunlop Volleys.
>
> Long before the modern jogger and all the fancy shoes for all the different sports and the different feet with the different soles and the different steps and so on (get exhausted just thinking about it now!) there was the Dunlop Volley.
>
> It was introduced by Dunlop Australia in 1939 and has had only minor changes to its design in over 70 years. Originally it was plain white but in the '70s a green and gold stripe was added to the heel.
>
> Aussie tennis players won many matches wearing them. Some of the more famous players to don the Dunlop Volleys were Rod Laver, Margaret Court, Evonne Goolagong, Ken Rosewall and Mark Edmondson.
>
> Mine always seemed to wear away in the same spot!

Dunlop Volleys, before Nikes and Reeboks.

Wikipedia, photo Edwinski

We always packed the alarm clock when travelling.

eBay

Once upon a time, when you were travelling, you always packed your travel alarm clock to make sure you knew the time and you woke up on time.

Imagine trying to explain to kids these days that you had to wind up the clock with a key (and be careful not to overwind because you might damage the spring), manually select the time you wanted the alarm to go off, wind up the alarm and everything was set.

All through the night you could hear the clock ticking away. Some had numbers that glowed in the dark so if you woke up you could check the time, and at the chosen time the alarm would sound, scaring the living bejesus out of you ... but at least you were awake on time!!

In the 1970s it seemed everything had to be orange and brown.

I vividly remember our kitchen back in the '70s and of course the colour was carried on through the other rooms as well.

I don't think we went for the orange wall or the floral orange wallpaper though.

Brown, I seem to recall, was very trendy in the lounge or family room. Wood panelling was at its height of popularity with a very tasteful orange and off-white vinyl lounge. Wood panelling eventually came to be detested in the late 1980s and early '90s and was looked upon as trashy. If you owned a home during this period, chances are you threw out the cheap composite panelling and re-painted the wall. It's easy to forget that it was once considered stylish.

Truth be told, I have to admit that I kind of like the ubiquitous brown.

It gave the decade a definite character – you can look at a 1970s interior and immediately tell that it's from that decade.

Today's decor doesn't quite have that trademark look. It's not as if we have all gone in our own bold directions; quite the opposite. It seems we've abandoned the crazy '60s psychedelic, the '70s brown and the '80s pastel in favour of ... what? Very conservative colours with stainless steel appliances and granite countertops.

'Bring back the brown,' I say!

What do you remember about the kitchen from that decade?

Kitchen wallpaper and accessories from the 1970s had lots of orange!

iStock

Robert Sanchez shared a photo: 'The mighty EH Holden is a bit of a legend in Australia. Whose family had one of these?

This Kodachrome slide was taken in 1965, when this EH was practically new. Another slide from the JC Collection.'

Sad to say that Holden's days as 'Australia's Own Car' are well and truly gone. On 11 December 2013, Holden announced that it would cease vehicle and engine production by the end of 2017. However, the company says it will continue to have a large and ongoing presence in Australia, importing and selling cars as a national sales company.

An EH Holden in 1965. The days when Holden was 'Australia's Own Car'.

Courtesy of Robert Sanchez at ReliveDigital

#24 FACT

The world's first seatbelt law was put in place in 1970, in the state of Victoria, making the wearing of a seatbelt compulsory for drivers and front-seat passengers. And by 1 January 1972, wearing seatbelts was compulsory throughout Australia. Not surprising considering that the death toll was down by almost 10 per cent in the first year after Victoria's world's first legislation.

The humble Aussie steak sandwich was a staple before the American-style fast-food chains arrived.

Courtesy of Andrew Heslop

Before the fast-food chains arrived in Australia, the old 'steak sandwich' was a bit of a staple.

Andrew Heslop shared a photo:

> It seems everyone is opening either a gourmet or healthy hamburger place these days – now including McDonald's® who are taking on hipster outlets like Grill'd.
>
> That puts the steak sandwich on the endangered list ... once a suburban staple along with an Aussie hamburger with the lot (which included an egg, slice of beetroot and also pineapple), meat pie and fish and chips.

Yep, can still recall the old-style hamburger with the egg and beetroot, and don't forget the tomato sauce on top!

Come to think of it, I haven't had a steak sandwich for years!

Phillip Adams wrote recently of the days of the local grocer:

> Oh for the days of the local grocer, when bread was white and cheese was Kraft – one of the few items that came in a pack. Everything else was bulk. Grandma would send the six-year-old me off with a list and the grocer would do the rest. Running up and down his ladder, slicing butter from the block. Biscuits (Milk Arrowroot mainly) were measured into paper bags – with broken bikkies given away in a cone of brown paper as a treat, an early version of the loyalty program. The bread was invariably High Tin, a loaf shaped like a bum. 'Don't pick the bread,' Nanny would warn me, but I always did on the way home, having parted the buttocks. And I remember the smell of that fresh bread!

Remember when the baker would deliver the bread, hot and still fresh, every day?

Pinterest

The American fast-food chain McDonald's arrived in Australia in 1971. It was almost immediately shortened to 'Maccas'.

McDonald's®

Back in 1971, McDonald's® opened its first restaurant in the Sydney suburb of Yagoona and changed forever Australia's fast-food eating habits.

My very first recollection of a McDonald's® Hamburger Restaurant was on the Central Coast of NSW in Gosford and that would have been in the mid-to-late '70s (I think it's still there).

Today there are over 900 McDonald's® across Australia and the company employs around 90 000 people across all its restaurants and management offices.

More than one million Aussies visit a McDonald's® restaurant every day.

Can you remember your first Big Mac?

I recall when writing a long composition with one of these school pens was a nightmare.

Museums Victoria. Reg. No: SH 940554

At school we wrote with a pen and nib, dipped constantly into the inkwell, and used a pink or white blotter to stop smudging.

The inkwells were topped up daily by the 'ink monitor'.

Ahhh, the kids of today don't know how easy they have it! Today's children will never know the agony of trying to finish homework with a crossed nib or when you dropped a blob of ink on your nearly finished assignment which the teacher was expecting to be 'neat and tidy'.

At school we were never allowed to use a fountain pen and the biro was considered to be the work of the devil by the nuns who taught me. What are your memories of doing school work with pen and ink?

I wonder how many of today's kids would even recognise this.

Yes, the card filing system that kept every office and company's business records together. Usually the responsibility of, and handled by, the office 'junior', it required constant and accurate updating.

With the computer technology available these days, card filing systems are no longer needed and the necessity for written records on cards, stored in alphabetical order, is another job that has now been long forgotten.

This was 'Googling it' back in the 1970s!

Wikipedia, photo Sailko

1973

Life in Australia before credit cards must have been very difficult!

Everyone was paid in cash and on payday you lined up to get your pay envelope. Then it was off to the bank, or to the various places where you owed money, to pay your bills in cash usually by lining up at the counter.

I think it may have been in the '70s that most companies started depositing your pay direct to a bank account, and then Bankcard came along. It was a shared-brand credit card issued by the financial institutions in Australia between 1974 and 2006.

Before 1974, only store cards, Diners Club and American Express were available in Australia and these were either restrictive or only accessible to the wealthy. Bankcard was eventually superseded by Visa and MasterCard and nowadays hardly anybody has much cash on them anymore.

Remember these old 'click-clack' machines? Now you simply wave your credit card at the terminal and everything is approved, no waiting.

An original 'click-clack' machine. Life changed dramatically when more easily available credit cards arrived in Australia in 1974.

eBay

#25 FACT

In 1902 Australia became the second country in the world, after New Zealand, to grant women suffrage, which approved the voting rights of women in 1893. South Australia enfranchised women in 1894, Western Australia did so in 1899, and the Australian Commonwealth government followed suit in 1902 (except for Aboriginal women). Australia also allowed women to seek election in parliament – our first female elected representative was Edith Cowan.

Before the days of internet banking, credit cards and ATMs, banks had many branches staffed by friendly tellers and there was no charge to actually walk into a bank.

Photo by News Ltd/Newspix

It might be hard to believe now, but there was a time when banks were very highly respected organisations and the bank manager was considered a leader in the community.

Back then the bank was the pillar of society and the local bank manager was held in the same regard as the local GP or priest. He was treasurer of the school committee, a member of the Rotary Club, and ran the bank branch as if it was his own business.

Many managers actually lived in a residence attached to the bank and knew all the regular customers by name. There was nothing competitive about banking in the '50s – even the advertising was genteel.

I remember that even in the '70s I had to have my manager assure the local bank manager that I had secure employment before I could get a mortgage!

The Dave Allen Show was a regular on Australian TV in the '70s and '80s.

One of my all-time favourite comedians! At the height of his career Allen was the most controversial comedian on British TV, regularly provoking indignation at his frequent highlighting of political hypocrisy and his disregard for religious authority.

Dave Allen always sat on a high bar stool facing the audience, smoking and occasionally sipping from a glass of what he always allowed people to assume was whiskey (in fact it was ginger ale with ice). He sometimes appeared deliberately crotchety and irritable on stage but always gave off an air of charm and serene melancholy both in his act and in real life.

Dave wrote most of his own gags and each day pored over newspapers, scribbling notes and ideas for his routines.

A genuinely funny comedian. He died in 2005.

Irish comedian David Tynan O'Mahony, better known as Dave Allen.

Alamy

Jamie Redfern was one of the most exciting young singers to emerge from the very successful TV program *Young Talent Time*.

Jamie was actually born in Liverpool in the UK so maybe there is something in the water there as suggested by the number of huge stars that come from that part of the world!

When he was three years of age, he would sing for the ladies in the street where he lived with ice cream as his reward. When the family moved to Australia his father encouraged him to audition for *Brian and the Juniors* or *Swallows Juniors*. He then become part of *Young Talent Time*.

Jamie was voted Australia's 'King of Pop' and best male vocalist, and was on numerous occasions called the best young singer and performer in the world by such legendary entertainment icons as Elvis Presley, Sammy Davis Junior, Johnny Carson, David Frost, Ginger Rogers, Roger Moore and Rock Hudson. Many American entertainers openly made it known that they believed the young Australian to possibly be the best boy singer and child performer of all time!

Jamie is currently a director of his singing school, appears on the club circuit and runs his own radio show.

Jamie Redfern first came to our notice as a talented young singer on *Young Talent Time*.

Festival Records

1976

When the Bay City Rollers came to Australia in 1976 they were mobbed by thousands of groupies. The fans went crazy!

The Bay City Rollers were a Scottish pop band whose popularity peaked in the mid-1970s. The *British Hit Singles & Albums* noted that they were 'tartan teen sensations from Edinburgh', and were 'the first of many acts heralded as the "biggest group since the Beatles" and one of the most screamed-at teeny-bopper acts of the 1970s'.

For a relatively brief but fervent period (nicknamed 'Rollermania'), they were worldwide teen idols. The group's line-up featured numerous changes over the years, but the classic line-up during its heyday included guitarists Eric Faulkner and Stuart John Wood, singer Les McKeown, bassist Alan Longmuir, and drummer Derek Longmuir.

Their 1976 appearance on *Countdown* coincided with a total eclipse of the sun. As thousands of fans bashed the Plexiglas studio doors desperate to gain entry, the sun eclipsed – the Rollers went up on the roof to witness it but the fans – unaware or afraid of losing their spot – didn't budge and missed that other once-in-a-lifetime experience!

The fans went crazy for the Bay City Rollers.

Bogaerts, Rob/Anefo, National Archives of the Netherlands

This Is Your Life was based on the American TV series of the same name and gave us a look behind the lives of the rich or famous.

TV Tonight

Remember the TV series *This Is Your Life*? I thought it was an excellent TV show. It was based on the American show of the same name, in which the host surprises famous guests with a show documenting their lives, with audience participation from their friends and family.

The show started in Australia in 1975 on the Channel 7 Network, hosted by Mike Willesee. (Subsequent seasons were compered by Digby Wolfe (1976) and Roger Climpson (1977–80).)

In 1995 the program was relaunched on the Nine Network, with a 13-year run, hosted by journalist Mike Munro. Then in November 2010, it was announced that the show would return to the Nine Network on 28 February 2011 and be hosted by Eddie McGuire. However, it was not as successful and after just four episodes the show did not return.

The Bee Gees have been around as a pop group for as long as I can remember. They started their careers back in 1958, as three young kids, brothers Barry, Robin and Maurice Gibb, and had their first big hit, 'Spicks and Specks', in 1966.

My first recollection of the trio is on *Bandstand* with Brian Henderson, singing 'My Old Man's a Dustman'.

They were originally born in Britain, got a start in Australia and returned to the UK in January 1967, where producer Robert Stigwood began promoting them to a worldwide audience.

One of the pop music industry's biggest success stories, the Bee Gees sold more than 220 million records worldwide, making them one of the world's best-selling music artists of all time. They were inducted into the Rock and Roll Hall of Fame in 1997.

Sadly Robin and Maurice have both died, leaving Barry as the sole survivor of the group.

The Bee Gees, Robin, Barry and Maurice Gibb, during their hugely successful career in the 1970s.

Alamy

One of the most successful pop groups Australia has ever produced is The Seekers.

The group was formed in 1962 by Athol Guy, who was joined by Keith Potger and Bruce Woodley. The three had all attended Melbourne Boys' High School together in the '50s.

Late in 1962 The Seekers met singer Judith Durham, who worked at the same advertising agency as Athol Guy. Born with perfect pitch, Judith originally planned to sing opera but she agreed to try singing folk music on the nights she wasn't playing jazz gigs.

And as they say, the rest is history!

The Seekers soon gathered a strong following, and Durham's connections with W&G Records led to the group being offered a contract. Their rise to fame and fortune began in 1963 when W&G released their debut album 'Introducing The Seekers', and there followed hit after hit.

You can still hear their most popular songs being played on the 'classic gold' radio stations today.

The Australian pop group The Seekers with Judy Durham.

Alamy

I hated sports day at school! I started wearing glasses at nine and was pretty awful at playing sport and would have rather read a book than taken part in competitive sport. But school sports day was a whole different and even more painful matter.

There would be 'novelty events' like the egg-and-spoon race, the three-legged race and the sack race. There would be a special participation event and everybody had to front up and take part, regardless of how bad you were. Our parents were invited to be present on the day too, which of course made it even worse. What are your memories of school sports day? Good or bad?

School sports day with 'novelty' events like the egg-and-spoon race and the three-legged race.

iStock

Who still reads the newspaper every day? Once upon a time the daily newspaper was the way we kept in touch with what was happening in our world. Newsagencies were sprinkled throughout the city and suburban areas. Newsboys and girls sold the last edition of the papers on city streets so we could get the latest as we caught the bus, train or tram on the way home.

Mostly all gone now. People now get their news via their smartphone, on a computer or tablet and newspaper mastheads are disappearing before our eyes.

I still have the newspaper delivered and read it every day with breakfast. I have the feeling though I am now in a minority group.

Most people started their day by reading a copy of the local newspaper.

Alamy

'I'm Louie the Fly, Louie the Fly, straight from rubbish tip to you.'

Courtesy of Mortein®

Considered by many people as the greatest advertising campaign ever devised in Australia, we've all grown up with Louie the Fly. Louie, the unlikely spokesinsect of Australian household insecticide brand Mortein®, first buzzed straight from the rubbish tip to you in 1957.

His TV career has spanned almost 60 years, providing daily reminders for Australians (no strangers to flies) that they and their families could get sick unless they keep a can of Mortein® on hand at all times.

In a jingle created by Bryce Courtenay and used in animated TV commercials since 1962, Louie proudly sings of his own dirtiness, claiming to be afraid of no-one except 'the man with the can of Mortein'.

#26 FACT

There are an estimated one million Arabian camels roaming wild throughout Australia's deserts – the largest number of purebred camels known in the world. And their numbers keep on increasing – it's thought that the population increases by about 8 per cent every year.

Remember these old 'flit' cans when you were trying to get rid of the flies and mozzies?

Courtesy of Gary Marsh

Gary Marsh shared a photo and memory from the distant past. 'Went to kill a blowie today and remembered the old pump-style fly sprayer. Who remembers these?'

I can't begin to imagine how toxic some of those old sprays were but the fly cans were the only type of thing we had to get rid of the mossies, flies and blowflies.

Just trying to remember, I think the liquid came in a brown coloured bottle which was poured into the fly can and then we'd spray away, covering everything, including ourselves, with a fine spray of liquid poison!

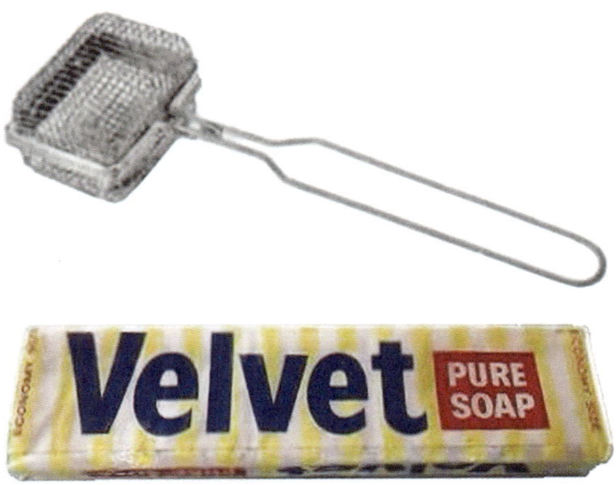

Before there was dishwashing liquid we used Velvet soap in a 'soap-saver'.

Courtesy of Ian Keith Kershaw

Ian Keith Kershaw sent a photo and posted some memories:

> Back before the early 1950s, there was no liquid detergent for washing kitchen dishes. A soap-saver (as shown) was used to hold pieces of hard soap and was shaken in the wash-up water to make it sudsy. Often a plain soap was cut and used, like the Velvet bar soap in the photo, as it wasn't highly perfumed like bath soap.
>
> Nothing was wasted back then.

Gosh, the old bar of Velvet soap brings pack a few memories.

Growing up during the Baby Boomer years, before mobile phones and a camera in every pocket, we all had a Kodak Instamatic Camera.

iStock

In a recent post, I asked what readers remember most about growing up in those Boomer years. Gail Hemmert wrote about red phone boxes. For Dean Wallbridge it was the milkman coming to the door and delivering bottled milk, soft drink bottles were refundable once empty, lollies were one cent, kids played outdoors, street cricket, neighbourhood parties, BBQ lunch and parties for footy finals. Audrey Challenor thought back to when the greengrocer came to the house with Vegies, Rawleighs sold Ointment, the spud truck would visit and if he stayed in the pub long enough ... spuds were free ... Milk came from the farmer and also meat. Kaye Cusack recalled 'when everything you bought was Australian made, you could leave a job on Friday and get a new one on Monday and you never heard of people getting stabbed, every kinder and primary school had Christmas activities'. And Kandy-Taline Fielding reminisced, 'You had to be home when the street lights came on ... Posting and receiving letters. Mixed lolly bags were .50c or less. No mobile phones with a camera in every pocket and no internet. As Mark Whetton commented, 'They were very special times back then'.

Did you ever ride the original Big Dipper at Luna Park in Sydney?

The Big Dipper was a wooden roller coaster ride that operated at Luna Park from 1935 until 1979. It was demolished in 1981.

It was first constructed in 1930 to an American design. Originally the wooden Big Dipper roller coaster was a mainstay of Luna Park Glenelg in South Australia during its four years of operation.

The ride was dismantled and shipped to Sydney when the Glenelg park went into voluntary liquidation in 1934, and became the biggest attraction of the newly opened Luna Park at Milsons Point.

Melbourne of course also has a famous Big Dipper and its own Luna Park.

The original big dipper at Luna Park in Sydney was dismantled and replaced in 1981.

State Library of New South Wales, 18043

Slim Dusty was the father of Australian country music, with a career spanning almost seven decades. He was the first Australian to have a No. 1 international hit song, with 'Pub with No Beer'. He received an unequalled 37 Golden Guitars and two Australian Recording Industry Association (ARIA) awards and was inducted into the Aria Hall of Fame and the Country Music Roll of Renown.

At the time of his death, at the age of 76, Slim had been working on his 106th album for EMI Records. In 2007, his domestic record sales in Australia surpassed seven million.

During his lifetime, Dusty was considered an Australian National Treasure. He performed 'Waltzing Matilda', Australia's national song, at the closing ceremony of the Sydney 2000 Olympic Games.

Slim Dusty was the first Australian to have an international hit with the iconic hit 'Pub with No Beer'.

Wikipedia, photo Charles John Ryman

Who do you think was the biggest Aussie larrikin when you were growing up? I reckon the first larrikin I can ever remember was Chips Rafferty who played the ocker role in many '50s and '60s movies.

A national survey conducted for News Ltd shows that 60 per cent of Australians think it would be a bad thing if our larrikin spirit vanished, while more than 30 per cent think it's already gone.

In the poll *Crocodile Dundee* star Paul Hogan was nominated as the man who best embodies the modern-day larrikin. Other larrikins nominated include Shane Warne, Hamish and Andy, and Hugh Jackman. Bob Hawke definitely qualifies I think and Shane Jacobson who played Kenny is high on my list too.

Actor Chips Rafferty was the first larrikin I can remember on the big screen.

Alamy

Who played with bubble pipes as a kid? I found this photo on Wikipedia and another one of a couple of bubble pipes on eBay and I was wondering if they can still be found. We always had bubble pipes as kids and I think you would make up a bit of soapy water, put a bit into the bottom of the bowl and blow out bubbles.

A pretty simple toy mainly used as a stocking filler at Christmas or in the 'lucky dip' at the school fete.

Most bubble pipes were made from plastic, so they couldn't be used for actual smoking. Usually brightly coloured, and sometimes featuring fanciful designs, they included multiple bowls.

Of course kids sometimes used bubble pipes in order to imitate the look of adults smoking.

Bubble pipes are now controversial because it is believed by some to encourage children to smoke later in life, similar to the controversy around lolly cigarettes.

Ah ... to be a kid again!

A girl blowing bubbles with a 'bubble pipe'. Remember?

Wikipedia, photo George Garrigues

When we went to the pictures there was an usherette to show us to our seats.

Picture theatres were such a big part of our lives as we grew up. On Saturday nights men would wear suits and ladies would be dressed to the nines for an evening out.

At that time there would have been more than a dozen people working in the theatre on any night: a manager, projectionists, an organist, ticket box staff, ushers and usherettes, refreshment counter staff, tray boys and cleaners.

I recently went to a multiplex cinema with six screens and there was one person collecting tickets (for all six theatres), two selling tickets and two behind the lolly counter – just five people running six theatres. Times have certainly changed!

An usherette from the Roxy Theatre, Parramatta in the '40s. Every picture theatre had ushers and usherettes who would shine a torch for you to get to your seat safely.

Pinterest

OPE
Flaming Beauty and
LAINE
EWART

1963

hoadley's
Polly Waffles
TEX
BAR
LUNCHEON
BAR
Paul walks off with the Show's best prize . . !
HOADLEY'S
CANDY
BARS

Tic-Toc biscuits were an after-school favourite at our house.

Bob Byrne

These were always an after-school treat at our house: Tic-Toc biscuits with a glass of milk or Milo, then a quick game outside before getting down to the serious business of homework.

They were also used to help kids learn how to tell the time. Each biscuit had a different time set on the face and before we were allowed to eat it we had to be able to tell what the time was. It was a very effective way of making us study and absorb how to read a clock. Today most children grow up with tablets, cell phones and laptops at their fingertips, all showing digital time, so perhaps they don't have to learn to read the old analogue clock as we did.

At Christmas there was a plastic Father Christmas at the top of the Christmas stocking.

Courtesy of Anthony Harrison

Anthony Harrison shared a photo that I'm sure will bring back some terrific memories for most: 'Here's something many people will remember, the header mask from the stocking that you'd receive from Father Christmas.'

Thank you, Anthony, that is a great memory for sure! I remember those Christmas stockings as a kid. They had a red net front and cardboard back and inside there were lots of small toys, things like a toy whistle, click-clacks, a mini comic and some lollies. Can you recall what else was included in those stockings?

#27 FACT

Moomba is Australia's largest free community festival held in Melbourne every year. It began in 1954 and Melburnians celebrated its 50th birthday in March 2005. The word 'Moomba' is an Aboriginal word meaning 'Let's get together and have fun.' Although some claim it actually means 'Up your bum'! And each year a new King and Queen of Moomba is crowned.

'What a funny old fellow is Humphrey'. Humphrey B Bear entertained and delighted kids on TV for more than four decades.

Ozpix Entertainment

Trent Mckinnon shared a post:

> *Here's Humphrey* was an Australian children's television series first aired on Monday 24 May 1965 on the Nine Network. It featured a character known as Humphrey B. Bear.
>
> First episode date: May 1965
> Final episode date: 2008
> Network: Nine Network
> Number of seasons: 40
> Awards: Logie Award for Most Outstanding Children's Program, Logie Award for Best Children's TV Series.

Thanks Trent. I read recently where there is now some discussion going on about finally giving Humphrey a voice. Humphrey may become a talking bear!

1969

Solvol in your bathroom gets really dirty hands clean fast.
Wash your hands Geoffrey...
...with the Solvol Geoffrey.
Amazing! You could eat your dinner off those hands.
SOLVOL
When you need more than just soap
SOLVOL
SOLVOL
Tough on dirt, gentle on hands, nothing cleans like Solvol.
It's creamy enough to keep in the bathroom but it's strong enough to shift grease, grime, Texta colours or football dirt from grubby hands, knees and elbows.
When you need more than just soap.
049 P 623
116

Reader Cate Louise shared a memory: 'Does anyone remember "Ripple Boots" in the '70s. I remember all the "tough" kids wore them in high school. If you were a girl that wore them, you were called a "ripple chick".' Thanks, Cate!

It was the 'rockers' who wore the ripple soles and to be authentic the boots had to have a certain number of ripples – 13 if my memory is correct. We wore them back in the '60s too and loved them when we were kids in high school, although we weren't allowed to wear them to school. I think we saw ourselves as teenagers with a bit of attitude. Duffle coats were around at the same time, in the era of bodgies and widgies. We thought we were so grown-up!

'When I was a teenager it was ripple sole DBs, denim jeans and black T-shirt with the durries up the sleeve.'

eBay

The 'ute' is actually an Aussie invention ... Back in the 1930s a Queensland farmer wrote to Henry Ford in the US, explaining that he couldn't afford to buy both a car and a truck. He explained that his wife thought the ideal vehicle would be one in which he could take his pigs to market and, at the same time, take her to town.

Henry Ford reportedly didn't warm to the idea at first, but put his design team on the job and they came up with a vehicle that was neither a car nor a truck but a sort of hybrid. Ford designer, Lew Bandt, developed the ute and the model was called a 'coupe utility'. Production started of the first Ford utes in 1934 and it took the country by storm.

Henry later wrote to the farmer thanking him for the idea, which revolutionised motor transport around the world.

This photo shows a 1964 Ford Falcon ute.

Another great Aussie invention, the 'ute'.

Wikipedia, photo GTHO

John Pattrick sent in a photo: 'Who remembers Smurfs from BP service stations for 89c each?'

Wow, John, that's quite a collection. I believe that BP started to sell or give away the Smurf figures in about 1979 and stopped selling them a couple of years later. BP garages used to give away Smurf figurines when petrol was bought.

Apparently the Smurf giveaway was a great success for BP, drawing in customers who waited patiently for each new release. It was in part responsible for the eventual popularity of the figures right around the world.

Smurfs have been around since the 1970s. This is a collection from the local BP service station.

Courtesy of John Pattrick

A gravity-fed petrol pump.

Courtesy of Shannon's Auctions

Before the '70s, petrol was served by an attendant at a service station from a gravity-fed petrol pump.

You had to know how to operate those pumps, unlike today where you just pull in, open your petrol cap, put the nozzle in and pull the trigger. And the attendant would also check your oil, radiator, tyre pressure and clean the windscreen for you.

Now it's all self-service, of course.

Golden Fleece petrol was sold in Australia from the 1920s but in the 1960s they introduced family restaurants at their service stations.

Car ownership in Australia ballooned after World War II and it proved to be a golden age for Golden Fleece. They expanded throughout the '50s and '60s and Golden Fleece service stations became roadhouse-style outlets with restaurants and bold signage.

After a whole day travelling with brothers and sisters in the back seat of the non-air conditioned car, the sight of the Golden Ram meant a stop, a pie with chips (eaten with knife and fork) and a Coke!

On a family road trip in the '60s we'd stop at a Golden Fleece service station and restaurant. They were the first to have 'roadhouses'.

Wikipedia, photo Bahnfrend

Remember when we had conductors on the buses, trams and trains to sell you one of these tickets and then punch it?

When I was a kid I always thought I'd like to be a conductor. They wore uniforms, collected all the money and back then, could kick you off the bus if you misbehaved.

What else could you ever want?

The tram or bus conductor would come along and punch your ticket.

Courtesy of Vintage and Allsorts

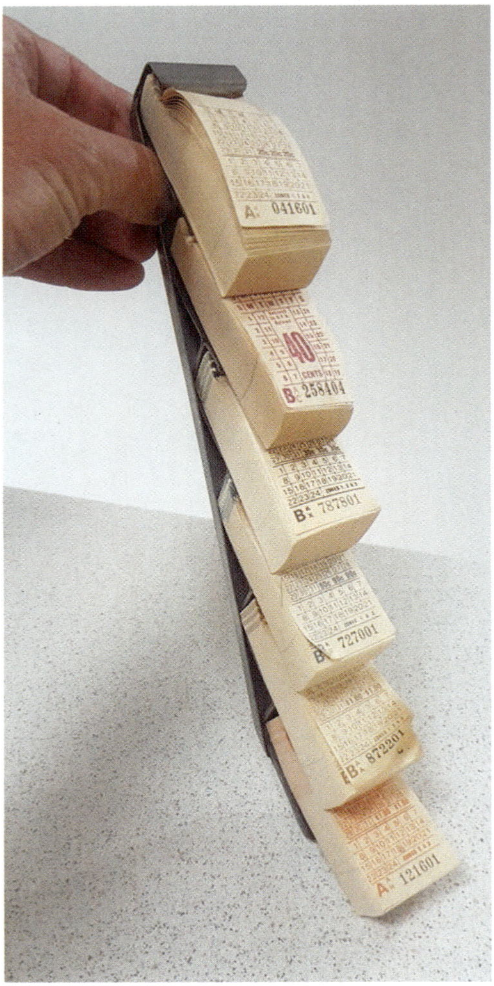

#28 FACT

Taking 1400 men eight years to build, the Sydney Harbour Bridge, nicknamed 'the Coathanger', is the widest long-span bridge and tallest steel arch bridge in the world. When it opened in 1932 it cost a car sixpence to cross and a horse and rider threepence. Originally it cost $4.2 million to build and took 55 years to pay off.

The toll gates on the Sydney Harbour Bridge were manned and you could even get change!

National Archives of Australia, A1200, L32700

It was only until recently – 2009 – that everyone had to stop at the toll gates and pay to cross the Sydney Harbour Bridge.

This photograph from the National Archives of Australia shows traffic flowing smoothly over the Bridge – once the city's worst bottleneck. Opened on 2 July 1959, two new lanes replaced the tram tracks on the east side, making eight in all.

New digital tolling was introduced onto the bridge in 2009 and the toll booths stood idle for about seven years before being finally removed in 2016.

Remember stopping to pay the bridge toll?

Such a simple little toy but very prized by all kids back in the day! Times were simpler then, of course, and toys were only ever given on two days of the year: your birthday and on Christmas Day.

There were four kids in our family, so each took a turn to get the toy at the bottom of the cereal box and we were never allowed to put our hand down into the corn flakes to see if we could find it either ... Big trouble if you were caught doing that!

Who remembers collecting these?

I loved finding the little toys in the bottom of the Corn Flakes packet. Do you recall finding one of these at the bottom of the Kellogg's Corn Flakes packet?

Pinterest

Knucklebones was a popular childhood game and played originally with real sheep knucklebones saved from the Sunday roast. 'Hygeinic' plastic 'jacks' soon followed.

Museums Victoria. Reg. No: SH 990053

Originally the game of knucklebones or jacks was played with real bones from the Sunday hogget (lamb) roast.

Sheep's knucklebones were the most common type of jacks in Australia during the first half of the last century, and children would colour them by boiling them in water with ink or dye.

During the 1950s, mass-produced plastic knucklebones became available. This photo, from 1954, is from the Museums Victoria collection and is an example of the very earliest type of mass-produced plastic replica knucklebones used by Australian children to play the game of jacks. The size, shape and weight of real sheep's knucklebones were replicated, in contrast to later versions, which are available these days, and are much smaller and lighter.

Did you ever have a plastic set?

A roll of caps for the cap gun. I vividly remember the smell.

Etsy

Anyone under 40 might have problem recognising this ... a roll of caps for a six-gun.

Loved playing Cowboys and Indians when I was a kid. Somehow I managed to get a Hopalong Cassidy outfit for Christmas one year and so was always one of the best-dressed cowboys. One of the other kids had an Indian headdress so we were often the leaders of the group. Boy, we had some big shootouts and dying from a bullet wound could take ages ...

I can still remember the smell after you fired the cap gun.

Spud guns were great fun! They were pistols that shot out little potato pellets. You'd just push the front of the gun into a potato and that would form a pellet. Essentially, spud guns were pipe-based guns that use air pressure or combustion to launch a projectile at a high speed.

You can probably guess that these would be considered very dangerous these days but we used to play with them when we were kids.

Playing with guns is not encouraged these days and that I can understand with all the violence in the world. Mind you, back in the '50s the world was just coming out of the horrors of World War II but there seemed to be a different attitude towards guns back then. We had cap guns as kids, slug guns as we got older and eventually .22 rifles and 303s for 'roo shooting.

Those potato pellets could really sting!

eBay

Construction of the Snowy Mountains Scheme – one of the greatest engineering and building projects ever undertaken in Australia – officially began on 17 October 1949. It took 25 years to build and once complete it cost $820 million dollars (equivalent to $10 billion in today's money).

Most of the workforce employed in the construction were immigrant workers who came to Australia under the 'Displaced Persons Scheme' which brought survivors from war-torn Europe to Australia but forced them to live and work for two years wherever they were sent by the government.

In an extraordinary feat these men constructed 1600 kilometres of roads and tracks. Seven townships and over 100 camps were built to enable the construction of the 16 major dams, seven hydroelectric power stations, two pumping stations, 145 kilometres of tunnel and 80 kilometres of pipelines and aqueducts. Just 2 per cent of the construction work is visible from above ground.

An underground tunnel being constructed for Snowy Mountains hydroelectric scheme at Cooma.

Photo by News Ltd/Newspix

#29 FACT

Based on the British program with the same name, *Play School* began production on 18 July 1966 (three years before *Sesame Street*). The first episode began transmitting that day, as the program went out live. It has been produced continuously since July 1966, making it the longest-running children's program on Australian TV. Big Ted, Little Ted and Jemima are still going strong.

Remember patty pans? Mum use to make little cakes and toffees for the school fete.

Courtesy of Anne Marie

Annie Marie shared this photo: 'This is a box of patty pans I have with original patty pans still in the box.'

Yes, they're patty pans and not cupcakes (as some people insist on calling them today).

Americanisms are more and more slowly but surely creeping into our everyday language. I heard someone on a TV news show recently refer to a baby's nappy as a diaper. Newspapers today have someone in jail instead of the gaol that we were taught in school and we're now getting cookies instead of biscuits.

I also find, when writing an article these days, it's easier to use the word 'program' instead of 'programme'.

I can remember my Mum using those patty pans to make little cakes and toffees for the school fete. Memories!!

The Mobile Public Library made sure that people in suburban and rural areas had access to books.

Alamy

When we were growing up in the '50s and '60s there was a mobile library that would regularly arrive and park in our suburban street so that both adults and kids could borrow books.

This would have been part of a local council or government scheme to ensure that people living in outer suburban or rural areas had access to books. Back in the day, not very many families had a car and bicycles were probably the main form of transport. Our mothers were stuck at home and the only means to get to a public library was via public transport so these mobile libraries were a godsend.

The mobile libraries kept our mothers in romance and mystery novels and the kids in Enid Blyton *Noddy* books and later *The Secret Seven* books.

Do you remember the mobile lending libraries from back then?

When fools are wise

"July, when wives philosophise, that fruit is soft, and fools are wise!"

All summer there are some soft fruits that make delicious fools. But July must be All-Fools' month! Only the young pink rhubarb has gone. Now we have yellow-green gooseberries, blackcurrants, redcurrants, crimson plums, purple damsons, raspberries, logan-berries, strawberries; all asking to be smoothed, creamed, sweetened into melting, mm-marvellous fruit fools.

Nestlé's is full-cream country milk and pure cane sugar; nothing but the very thing! And concentrated to just the consistency to make a perfect fool of any tart, sharp-tasting fruit. It's almost *too* easy. Simply whip it: you won't beat it.

FOOL PROOF

You will need, for 2 to 3 people:—

½ pint fruit purée, unsweetened. That is, fruit stewed down without sugar, until it is thick; and then sieved.

4 to 5 tablespoons of Nestlé's Milk.

Colouring, if liked.

Savoy, or Sponge Fingers.

Whip the fruit purée into the Nestlé's Milk. Add the colouring. Put into individual glasses, and prettify the tops as you please. Serve a sponge finger with each.

**This is just one from scores of "Favourite Recipes", which Nestlé's will be happy to send you FREE, if you write to The Nestlé Company Ltd. (Dept. 27), Hayes, Middlesex.*

Nestlé's Milk

RICHEST IN CREAM

*Such as Chocolate Fudge, Lemon Meringue Pie, Satin Creams, Dundee Cake: all far nicer and more nourishing made with Nestlé's Milk.

School lunch was wrapped in greaseproof paper and placed in a well-used brown paper bag, which then sat in the Globite school case until lunchtime.

National Archives of Australia

Seeing that ad for Nestlé condensed milk brought back memories of how much we loved the stuff as kids. I recall that we used to secretly buy a tin, smuggle it into the bedroom, punch two holes in the top and lie in bed and suck the sweet gooey liquid before going off to sleep. You could also buy it in a tube. It's a wonder I have any teeth left at all!!

Do you remember buying condensed milk and scoffing the whole can or tube?

Nestlé's milk ... Hmmmm!

Alamy

Back in the day, we ate school lunch straight from a school case or school bag.

Sandwiches were usually wrapped in greaseproof paper inside a brown paper bag and you could never get rid of that food smell from inside the school case or bag.

There were no insulated lunchboxes or cooler bags back then to keep everything cool so any perishable food just sat inside the case or bag on the hottest of days. How we did not get botulism or food poisoning on 40-degree days I don't know.

What with drinking warm milk at morning recess and then eating improperly stored food at lunch it's a wonder any of us survived our school days! But we did.

All the lolly jars lined up on the counter and a shilling would get you a big bag.

Flickr

Natalie Hausler shared a photo: 'Remember the great Aussie sleepout? Attached to a lot of old homes back in the '50s and '60s. This was my Nan and Pop's in Glandore in SA.'

Thanks, Natalie, that brings back memories – trying to sleep in the sleepout on a stinking hot night, no air conditioning and no electric fans. I imagine there would have been very little thought given to any insulation; sleepouts were sort of asbestos lean-tos really, with those louvred windows, they converted the veranda area into an extra room for one or two of the kids.

Also sometimes used (in our house at least) as a sewing room for Mum and the place where Dad would store the homemade ginger beer. You'd sometimes hear a few corks pop at 3 o'clock in the morning!

The sleepout was usually a converted veranda area constructed with asbestos sheeting that created an extra room for some of the kids.

Courtesy of Natalie Hausler

The lolly jars would sit on the front counter at the local milk bar or corner shop and for threepence or sixpence you could buy a little white paper bag full of your favourite lollies.

Musk Sticks, Licorice Blocks, Mint Leaves, Milk Bottles, Clinkers, Snakes Alive, Strawberries and Creams, Jelly Beans, Red and Green Frogs, Conversation Lollies, Cobbers, Freckles, Gobstoppers or Choo Choo Bars, Chokito bars, Kool Mints, Rosy Apples, Redskins, Scorched Peanut Bars, Killer Pythons, Turkish Delight, Crunchie Bars, Bullets, Cherry Ripe, Cadbury's Milk Chocolate and Darrell Lea liquorice and Rocklea Road were among the perennial favourites!

Did I leave anything out?

I was thinking this morning as I jumped out of a warm bed to step into a warmed bathroom and turned on the instant hot water system, how easy we have it these days.

When I was growing up there would have been no heater in the bathroom and hot water would have required the chip heater to be stoked and lit.

The wood stove in the kitchen would also have to be lit using newspaper and kindling before putting in the wood, just to make a pot of tea. There was no hot water without fire back then and that meant wood would have to have been chopped the day before and the fire started and the oven warmed up before you could put the kettle on.

We had a big woodheap down by the back fence and it was a haven for all sorts of creepy crawlies, lizards and the occasional snake.

Several times throughout the year, the wood man would deliver a big truck load of various sized logs, which then had to be neatly stacked (Oh, the splinters!) and covered with a tarpaulin as protection from the rain.

It was my job to cut the kindling, which required me to use a sharp axe and I can never recall wearing safety glasses or in fact any sort of protective clothing.

Remember the old wood chip heaters in the bathroom?

A chip heater. In winter Dad used to set it the night before so he didn't have to wait in the cold bathroom while it heated the freezing cold water.

432 Pages

Back in the '70s someone came up with the brilliant idea of turning your old newspapers and cardboard into combustible bricks to burn in the fireplace.

You had to soak the newspapers in a bucket of water until they became a soggy mess, then tear them into strips which you placed inside the brickmaker, compress and allow 24 hours to dry, remove from the brickmaker and allow to dry out completely before throwing them on the fire.

I love telling the story about how our whole family pitched in helping to tear the newspapers into strips, went through the whole process and at the end of the first week ended up with seven bricks. On Saturday night, we lit the fire and threw in the first brick – WHOOSH, it went up in three minutes flat!

The seven bricks lasted for less than half an hour and it was back to burning wood. We sat around and laughed until we almost cried. It took a whole week to produce about half an hour of fire. LOL!

It seemed like such a good idea at the time ... turning your old newspapers into paper bricks to burn on the fire.

shoptick.co.uk

Do you have the *Women's Weekly* recipe cards box at your house? Or your mum's or your aunty's house?

Courtesy of Richard Donnelly

Richard Donelly sent me this photo to share of the *Women's Weekly* recipe cards. Thanks, Richard!

Pip Lincolne on her blog 'Meet Me at Mikes' recently wrote:

> Did you have these cards in your house when you were a wee person? I did. I thought they were GREAT. I cooked lots of things from these cards as a child and a teenager. My parents used these cards too. This yellow box was the Kitchen Oracle at my house and we flipped through the cards with more anticipation than a swap card session in the playground.

Remember the *Australian Women's Weekly* recipe cards when you were growing up?

The Slinky is able to perform a number of tricks, like 'walking' down a flight of steps end-over-end as it stretches and re-forms itself, pulled by gravity and its own momentum. It can also appear to levitate for moments after it's been dropped. Slinkies were a big thing in the late-'60s to early '80s and we'd have Slinky races and see how far you could get them to go; they were lots of fun for very little price.

Other slinky toys include the Slinky dog; Loco, the Slinky train; Suzie, the Slinky worm; and the Slinky Crazy Eyes – a pair of glasses with Slinkys over the eyeholes with plastic eyeballs attached.

A toy favourite in the 1970s and '80s was the Slinky.

iStock

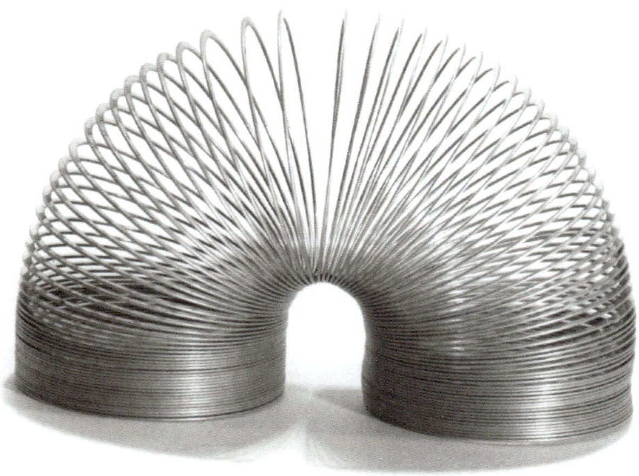

Slingshots were banned by our parents and school but it never stopped us from making and owning one. Thinking back, they were a very dangerous toy.

Museums Victoria. Reg. No: SH 990097

Who had a shanghai (slingshot) as a kid? Growing up in the '50s and '60s we'd make our own. We'd go looking for special forked sticks and we'd get the old car inner tubes and cut them up into thin straps or just use rubber bands and then we'd get some old leather to hold the gibbers (little stones) and we'd chase each other shooting the gibbers at each other. I think about it now and I shudder to think what could have happened. Of course we got in trouble if we were caught and they'd be taken away from us, but we'd go and make them all over again!

There were always games to play in the schoolyard at recess and lunchtime. Here's a group engaged in a serious game of Bob Down Tiggy.

Museums Victoria. Reg. No: MM 104101/ Photographer: Dr Dorothy Howard. Courtesy of Dr June Factor

According to the *Daily Mail Australia* recently, schools are being urged to bring back traditional playground games to combat childhood obesity.

Chasey or tag, British Bulldog, What's the time, Mr Wolf? and oranges and lemons are on the list of recommended games to play at break-time, as well as hopscotch, skipping, hide-and-seek, French elastic and marbles.

But who remembers the game Bob Down Tiggy?

This photo is one of a group of photographs probably taken by American folklorist Dr Dorothy Howard while she was studying children's games and playlore in Australia.

The photo shows nine boys playing 'Bob Down Tiggy' in a government school playground in Melbourne. The boys are in a rough circle, with three boys bobbing down, others half-crouching or standing. I can't ever recall playing this game, can you?

#30 FACT

Adelaide is known as Australia's wine capital. Producing near half of the country's yearly wine total, South Australia is home to 18 different wine regions and more than 200 cellar doors, all within just an hour's drive of the city.

We'll drink to that.

Ian Keith Kershaw sent a photo to share: 'Remember when the PMG used to have red pillar boxes for you to post your mail?

This rare relic is still in use by Australia Post!'

Thanks, Ian. I started my working life at the age of 14 as a telegram boy working for the PMG Dept (now Australia Post). Part of my job was to 'do the pillars', which was to clear all the letters from these post boxes twice a day, Monday to Friday at 10 am and 4 pm. We used to ride a bike back then so it was uphill and down dale on my red PMG bike (number 2417) to make sure the mail got through.

The red colour became so well known that you'd often hear people refer to a bright red colour as 'pillar box red'.

Those were the days when letter writing was at its most popular. It was the most common means of communication between family and friends. I recall my mother writing letters every week to her mother, brothers and sister as well as regular letters to close relatives and friends.

It's hard to appreciate in these days of instant communication that it could take over a week or more for a letter to be delivered.

Who remembers when we had these red post poxes on just about every second corner in every city and country town across Australia?

These bright red post boxes were dotted everywhere throughout Australian cities, suburbs and country towns. Very few remain.

Courtesy of Ian Keith Kershaw

AUSTRALIA
POST
NEWSPAPERS

It was something almost every family did at least once on a drive through Victoria: visit the Fletcher Jones Factory and Gardens.

Throughout the '30s and '40s FJ stores were opened around Australia, selling men's suits and trousers. In 1947, David Fletcher Jones purchased a large plot of land in Warrnambool and erected a purpose-built factory surrounded by beautiful gardens to cater to his successfully growing business.

The 1970s and '80s were the 'golden years' of Fletcher Jones with stores located across the breadth of Australia and manufacturing centres in Warrnambool and Mt. Gambier employing approximately 3000 people. The factory closed many years ago and fell into a state of disrepair but has recently been restored and is now a market and once again the pride of Warrnambool.

When our mums went shopping it was usually with the string bag. No plastic bags back then.

The Vintage Knitting Lady, www.thevintageknittinglady.co.uk

My mother, and I'm sure that most of our mothers, used a string bag when they went shopping. No plastic bags back then and the string bag was easy to carry around and was expandable.

Now I believe string bags are making a comeback.

My wife has bought one of the new string bags that folds neatly into a small purse: easy to carry, flexible and convenient.

Sometimes it's worth looking again at some of the things used by those generations before us – you just never know what you'll find.

Fletcher Jones Factory and Gardens in Warrnambool.

Courtesy of Adam Dimech

BESTWAY
LEAFLET 3d.
861
STRING SHOPPING BAGS
In Knitting and Crochet

Leigh Roberts posted a question: 'Does anybody "remember when" in the early '60s you could play a quiz whilst traveling in the car from cards that you could get from either BP or Golden Fleece servos? You had to tick off certain items found or seen. Hope someone else remembers ...'

Yes, Leigh, you're probably thinking of BP SPOTTO.

In the late 1950s and early 1960s we would go to various places in my Dad's 1958 Zephyr Mark 2, playing Spotto for hours to keep us kids amused on the long trip, although yelling out 'SPOTTO bike' or whatever did get a bit loud sometimes!

My early memories also include, as a very young child, being on the bus or train as we didn't have a car then. Later when we had the car, it was 'I spy with my little eye' or 'Riddle me riddle me ree' or Spotto, followed by 'Are we there yet? Are we there yet?'

Back then we pretty much made up our own games with a bit of imagination and inventiveness!

When my children take their children on a trip now it's all iPhones, iPads, portable DVD players and iPods.

BP Spotto was a favourite to keep the kids entertained on the long road trips.

Bob Byrne

Before air-conditioned cars arrived we had a window vent to direct air flow into the car.

Wikipedia, photo Christopher Ziemnowicz

Just talking about some of the joys of motoring back in the day. Roy Sheppard sent in this photo of the window side vent.

You'll never see these on modern cars, of course, because they're all fully air-conditioned and there's no need to open the windows.

When I first started driving in the late '50s there was no air-conditioning except for the four windows. I can remember road trips in the old '49 Austin A40 on a 40-degree day and the air coming into the car was like from a blast furnace ... but it was the only way of getting air into the car. Funnily enough I still drive with my windows down on a hot day even though I have an air-conditioned car. I still prefer the fresh (usually hot) air to turning on the air con. How about you?

In the 1950s, many little girls dreamt of owning a bride doll.

In her book about growing up, *Depicting Canada's Children*, Loren Lerner remembers that her bride doll spent most of the time in a cardboard box with a cellophane window. As the most prized of dolls she was only taken out and played with on special occasions. Loren also makes the point that the bride doll is still in her family and has been passed on to the next generation.

Just a quick check on eBay shows that these vintage bride dolls are now in demand and fetching up to $150.

Do you still have your bride doll?

Almost every little girl wanted her own bride doll.

eBay

First Communion was usually followed by the First Communion breakfast.

Shutterstock

One of the rituals I remember as a kid growing up a Catholic was the First Holy Communion.

Traditionally, First Communion was an important event – often ending in a large family gathering to celebrate.

Girls usually wore a white dress with a white veil. And boys would wear a new suit, especially bought for the occasion. Religious gifts – such as rosary beads prayer books, religious statues and holy cards – were given. Cash was common too, and much more preferred!

I think the nuns started getting us ready for the big day about a year beforehand. We had to learn all about this thin little wafer of bread becoming the body and blood of Christ, which you had to swallow but weren't allow to chew (under pain of going to Hell). It was a big social event too, with the First Communion breakfast for all the kids afterwards.

I'm not sure what the Protestants made of it all, but strangely, even though it seemed the nuns and the priests didn't like the Protestants very much, I got along with them very well.

Remember your First Communion?

Back in the day when everyone knew what you meant by 'spending a penny'.

Courtesy of 'The Vintage Wall'

When 'spending a penny' meant you really had to spend a penny!

Back in the '50s and early '60s almost all public lavatories required a penny in the slot so you could open the door to do your business. The penny would no doubt have gone towards the upkeep and cleaning costs and some lavatories had an attendant who would hand you a small towel while keeping everything clean and tidy.

They were called lavatories back in the day. Not sure when the word 'toilet' came into use in Australia.

Charging to use a public toilet these days would be seen as discriminatory.

Who wishes you could still buy one of those incinerators and have a big burn-up?

Just $14.95 with free delivery and installation, tidy and neat, hygenic and handy, with neighbour harmony guaranteed as there were no cinders!

My recollection is that there was always a neighbour who stoked up and lit the incinerator when the washing was hanging out on the line. It wasn't just the cinders but the smoky smell that lingered on your clothes and bedding for a week.

No more trips to the tip! Ahhh, the good old days!

Two things the great Aussie backyard was famous for – backyard cricket, and there was nothing more satisfying that having a big 'burn-up' in your own backyard incinerator.

Courtesy of Lisa Marker

#31 FACT

When the Queensland Parliament was built it didn't include women's toilets. When Irene Maud Longman, the first female MP in parliament, had to use the facilities she had to leave her shoes out the front of the door to let everyone know she was inside. That was in the year 1929.

Back in the day most lavatories were outside and the first flush toilets were high tank with a pull handle on a chain.

Courtesy of Bronwyn Lewis

They were called 'high tank' toilets.

This photo takes me back to my early teenage years when the first flush toilets were introduced. My family lived in a large industrial town and we didn't have the sewer or septic tanks until the '60s. Before that we had a pan system (when the night cart man changed the pan every week) or a 'long drop'.

The last time I visited a 'long drop' was at a national park in the Northern Territory while on holidays. The smell was overpowering!

How on earth did we survive pans and long drops before flush toilets arrived?

Before the fast-food chains arrived we used to love a banana sundae at the local milk bar.

iStock

Peter Russell-Clarke was one of the first television chefs and hosted a five-minute show in the 1970s called *Come and Get It*, which aired on ABC TV for nine years. Peter was making his name as a personality in the kitchen long before chefs and cooking shows became all the rage.

Peter also wrote and published several cookbooks and books about food.

In the period 1975 to 1979, Russell-Clarke was the spokesman in several highly successful and much discussed campaigns on behalf of the Victorian Egg Board and the Australian Dairy Corporation. Victorian egg sales rose 5 per cent in three years.

He frequently used the catchphrase 'G'day' at the start of segments of *Come and Get It*.

Remember his laughing 'G'day' at the beginning of each segment?

Photo by News Ltd/Newspix

I'm sure kids would still love them today but when I was a kid and even a teenager, I used to love 'banana split sundaes'.

These and milkshakes were the favourite at the local milk bar or deli after school or on the weekends.

There's a much wider choice these days of course and the humble banana split probably doesn't quite have the same following as some of the newer dessert delights from the fast-food chains but back in the day it was the number one taste sensation!

I remember they were usually served in a glass boat dish and had three scoops of ice cream, banana or chocolate topping and nuts and a glacé cherry on top. Delicious ...

Remember hoeing into one of these?

A NewSouth book

Published by
NewSouth Publishing
University of New South Wales Press Ltd
University of New South Wales
Sydney NSW 2052
AUSTRALIA
newsouthpublishing.com

First published 2018

10 9 8 7 6 5 4 3 2 1

ISBN 9781742236148 (paperback)

NATIONAL LIBRARY OF AUSTRALIA A catalogue record for this book is available from the National Library of Australia

Design Josephine Pajor-Markus
Front cover Our parents encouraged us to become Boy Scouts and Girl Guides. National Archives of Australia; Kitchen wallpaper and accessories from the 1970s had lots of orange! iStock; The best birthday parties had fairy bread and lots of raspberry cordial! thecattylife.com; The toll gates on the Sydney Harbour Bridge were manned and you could even get change! National Archives of Australia. *Back cover* When my wife and I got married in the 1970s she had a 'glory box' and in it were all the vital things we needed to set up our new home. Courtesy Bauer Media Pty Limited/*The Australian Women's Weekly*; Clag came with its own brush, which was attached to the lid. Pinterest; Saturday matinee at the pictures with ice cream and lolly trays at interval. Alamy; These moon rockets were very popular in playgrounds from the '60s through to the '90s but were removed because of safety concerns. Wikipedia, photo Sladew; Tic-Toc biscuits were an after-school favourite at our house. Bob Byrne
Printed in China

This book is printed on paper using fibre supplied from plantation or stainably managed forests.

UNSW SYDNEY